THE
WORLD
OF
SAMUEL
ADAMS

by

Donald Barr Chidsey

THOMAS NELSON INC., PUBLISHERS
Nashville, Tenn. • New York, New York

First edition

Library of Congress Cataloging in Publication Data

Chidsey, Donald Barr.
    The world of Samuel Adams.

    SUMMARY: A biography of the patriot and politician whose speeches, writings, and activities, including the Boston Tea Party, helped stir up the colonists against Great Britain.
    Bibliography: p.
    1. Adams, Samuel, 1722–1803.   2. United States—History—Revolution.   [1. Adams, Samuel, 1722–1803.   2. Statesmen, American.   3. United States—History—Revolution]   I. Title.
E302.6.A2C47   973.3'092'4   [B]   [92]   74–698
ISBN 0–8407–6383–2   Feb. 13, 1975

Contents

The World of Samuel Adams

CHAPTER ONE

First in Connivance

A more unlikely Founding Father it would be hard to imagine. Samuel Adams, in appearance, was an extraordinarily ordinary man, a man unskillfully put together. The Marquis de Lafayette has been described as a statue wandering around looking for a pedestal to stand on, but this picture would never apply to Samuel Adams, who could not have graced any high place. He was thin and pale, had a sallow complexion, wishy-washy gray eyes, and a throat all cords. He wore clothes that were drab and sloppy. His lips twitched and trembled, for he suffered from palsy, and his hands were seldom still.

Thomas Hutchinson, the last civilian royal governor of Massachusetts and Samuel Adams' dearest enemy, was wont to call him the Machiavel of Chaos; yet his manner was quiet, kindly, and low-keyed, and he never forgot that he was a Harvard man.

History has labeled him the Great Rabble-Rouser, but one with a high, reedy voice like his—a voice that quavered when he raised it—could not truly have been a rabble-rouser. He might more accurately be dubbed the originator of American machine politics. He never stood on a stump. He would speak from the floor of a legislative chamber whenever he thought that a speech was called for, but he abjured magniloquent periods, and when he was finished, he sat down. Classical allusions came out of him readily, for he *thought* in terms of ancient Greece and Rome, especially Rome, which was as real to him as the cobblestones he trod on the street—he never could afford a horse. But classical allusions were the bread and butter of eighteenth-century elocution and were not in themselves a sign of pomposity.

This man had courage. He virtually invented independence in America. Before his time it had been a dirty word. He brought it respectability; indeed, he brought it life.

His figure is sinister only in retrospect. Today we would designate him as a rigger, a schemer who toiled behind the political scenes. His associates praised him as a master worker "out-of-doors." It was a phrase of the time, and not pejorative. To work out-of-doors meant to get things lined up before your political opponents could do so, to have one's course charted before the opening gavel banged against its block. It meant buttonholing, whispering promises, half-breathing threats. Had legislative buildings been equipped with lobbies then, Samuel Adams would have been hailed as the first great lobbyist. But he could work indoors as well, and did. He served on all sorts of committees, for he knew by instinct and training alike that to succeed in politics a man must work hard and, more important, persistently. Adams took no vacation, knew no holiday. He was always there, a boll weevil.

He was not serpentine, but was a straightforward thinker who eschewed rhetorical flourishes. His words never wobbled; there was no touch of the weasel in them. He saw his fight and faced it. The royal charter that had been granted to the colonists of Massachusetts Bay was being violated by the English ministers of the Crown, and this violation must be resisted. It was as simple as that. The rights of his fellow countrymen—their inalienable rights as Englishmen—were about to be taken from them. This must not be permitted. He, Samuel Adams, was not a radical, heaven forbid. The Tories were the radicals. *He* stood foursquare for the rights and privileges that the residents of Massachusetts province had been promised, and he would continue to stand for them.

Though he might sometimes be described as "devious," there was nothing "shady" about Samuel Adams. Nobody ever accused him of being dishonest, or even dreamed of such a thing. Of the thirteen Atlantic-coast colonies, Massachusetts, which then embraced Maine, was by far the foremost in its demands for more self-government and eventually for freedom. Massachusetts led the others. And Boston led Massachusetts. Samuel Adams, as a result of many years of silent, dogged work, when the crisis came led Boston.

It was an age of cynicism, of nepotism, when bribery was rampant, and even accepted. The King's party undoubtedly approached the leader of the Massachusetts dissidents with tempting offers. Perhaps Samuel Adams did not even understand them. He might have become rich. A nod of his head would have done it. Despite his blatantly unaristocratic appearance, he might have been made a baronet or at least a knight. It never occurred to him.

Indeed he flaunted his poverty as if it were some sort of proud polychromatic oriflamme symbolic of his cause. Of the various municipal and provincial jobs he held, only one, the clerkship of the General Court of Massachusetts, paid a salary, and that varied, though it averaged less than £100 a year. Neighbors from time to time would pitch in and paint or otherwise repair Adams' rambling old house in Purchase Street, lest it fall apart. Sometimes too, thinking of the children, they would send over food. Samuel Adams scarcely seemed to be aware of these things.

He has been called the Last Puritan, but that is ridiculous. Probably we will never see the last Puritan. Samuel Adams was, however, a *pure* Puritan. Doubt never grazed his consciousness. Today's popular picture of Puritanism includes sniveling and a liberal dash of holier-than-thou—that is, hypocrisy. Such was never the case with Samuel Adams. Everybody who knew him knew where he stood, and he was as firm as Gibraltar. To be sure, there were prayers every morn-

ing in Purchase Street, as there were Bible readings every
night after supper, and the whole family went to the Old
South Church twice on Sunday. That did not keep the clerk
of the General Court from bargaining for votes, and getting
them, in the Bunch of Grapes, the Green Dragon, and the
Salutation Tavern.

He longed for the clean, stern, sturdy days of Cotton
Mather, of Jonathan Edwards. He truly believed that the
people of Boston, properly guided, could be caused to resume
those old ways that had been so good for the soul.

He made mincemeat of his enemies. It was he, for example,
who poniarded England with the epithet "a nation of shopkeepers," a phrase sometimes attributed to Napoleon Bona-
parte, who was only seven years old when Samuel Adams
used it in a speech in Philadelphia. Even those who disliked
him marveled at his skill in parliamentary maneuvering and
regarded him as a practitioner of the immediate, the real; and
they would have been amazed to learn that in fact the man
lived most of his life in the Rome of the Caesars, a place to
him always more real than Massachusetts. Of English history
he knew little, but of the Eternal City he knew everything
that a scholar could. The fall of that world empire was a
personal matter to him, a cause of deep, bitter concern, for he
was convinced that it had been the work of the Devil, and he
could see all around him signs of a second such fall. A return
to the faith of our fathers was what was needed, and this
urgency tugged at him.

He was a politician. It has been pointed out that such men
are as much needed as are undertakers or the collectors of
rubbish. *Somebody* must do that work. Samuel Adams did it
supremely well.

Washington has been hailed as the Father of his Country,
but it would not be irreverent, nor yet inaccurate, to call
Samuel Adams the grandfather. He was the one who laid the
foundation.

CHAPTER TWO

Town Meeting, with Embellishments

The Adamses were a cantankerous lot, crusty parties all of them. The pugnacious second President of the United States burned with indignation at all times. He was a pudgy bundle of irascibility, who was sometimes referred to, from his figure, which was clownish, as His Rotundity. A doughty battler for the Lord, John Adams had a bald spot, and popping, damn-you eyes, and when he walked, he waddled. The silliest thing about him was his mouth, which was that of a woman who pouts. He was a brilliant lawyer, but in appearance preposterous. His son, John Quincy Adams, virtually made a career of oppugnancy; there was nothing that he didn't excoriate; he must have carried lemon juice in his mouth instead of spit. His words withered whatever they struck, and his manner repelled. It was, seemingly, a family trait. As late as the early part of this century John Hay, then secretary of state in Washington, used to call his friend Henry Adams, the historian, great-grandson of John I, Porcupinus Angelicus.

This, however, was the Braintree branch of the family. Samuel Adams came from Boston proper, a city in the early 1760's of slightly over fifteen thousand and the biggest port in America. There was nothing of the curmudgeon about

13

him. He made friends easily. He was always ready to listen to anybody. His speaking voice was even enough, if a mite high, but his "speeching" voice tended to squeak. His *singing* voice, on the other hand, was pleasant, a high, lilting tenor. Samuel Adams loved to sing. It must not be supposed, however, that the taverns and other meeting places where he was known, and where he mapped the future of a nation, sheltered Heidelberg-type sessions. Beer did flow on these occasions, while men puffed at their churchwardens, but no songs rose. In the Bunch of Grapes or in Vernon's Head the talk was too momentous to be interrupted by vocalization. When Samuel Adams sang, it was in his own home or the home of a friend, and never of course on the Sabbath.

Samuel Adams of Boston and John Adams of Braintree shared a great-great-grandfather, Henry, a farmer in Devonshire, England, though the family is supposed to have originated in Wales. Henry Adams was the first of that name in Massachusetts; he crossed in 1636. Samuel and John, then, were second cousins. Samuel was the older by thirteen years, almost to the day, and already was a prominent figure in public life when John from Braintree first blustered his way into Massachusetts politics. John, at no time unaware of his own resounding abilities, was not ordinarily the type who looked up to others, but he did look up to Samuel, of whom he was in awe, and was habitually respectful to him. They worked well in harness. Samuel was the more approachable, as he was the more advanced, the more daring—an innovator. John simply never could understand the older man, who, though a writer, had no trace of vanity, a quality with which John was surcharged.

Both went to Harvard, where at the time it was the custom to rate all students numerically in the order of the social and economic importance of their families. Samuel Adams in a class of fifty-two was rated five, but John Adams, some years later, and in a slightly larger class, was rated only fifteen.

John's mother had been a Boylston, true, but Samuel's mother had been a Fifield, and that must have made the difference.

Samuel was born September 16, 1722, at twelve o'clock noon. It was a Sunday. His father, also named Samuel, usually was known by his title of Deacon. *Père* and *fils* alike were poor businessmen. The deacon got involved in an elaborate soft-money scheme, a Massachusetts land bank that the provincial government quite properly sat on. Samuel, Jr., had always taken poverty for granted. At Harvard he waited on table to help pay his way. He was in the class of '40. Three years later he got his master's degree.

When Calvin Coolidge came to the White House, Will Rogers suggested that he fill out the "occupation" blank in the entrance form with "officeholder." It was so with the Samuel Adamses, father and son. They always managed to be on the public payroll.

Deacon Adams was, at different times, a tithingman, a constable, an assessor, a selectman, and a representative in the General Court, the lower house of the provincial assembly. He was also, for a short time, the hogreeve, though few pigs any longer roamed the streets of Boston. He was one of the founders of the Caucus Club.

Authorities differ as to the origin of the name, and some say that it was first known as the Calkers' Club. Undeniably calkers and other kinds of shipbuilders—ropemakers, joiners, sailmakers, shipwrights—made up most of the club's early membership. It was among just such people that the power of Samuel *père* was most firmly seated; his name always was huzzahed along the waterfront. Samuel Adams, Jr., did not inherit this leadership intact; he had to work for it. The Caucus clubs (there were soon to be three of them, the North End, the Middle, and the South End) controlled Boston politically, and young Samuel controlled the Caucus clubs.

Deacon Adams' means had been lessened by the land-bank scheme, but not wiped out. When the son was graduated from Harvard, the father was able to advance him some £200 to set him up in the merchandising business, but the youth went through this, leaving nothing. Not that he was a wastrel! Waste, in his eyes, would be classed with sloth, gluttony, avarice. The trouble was, he had no instinct for business. Trusting everybody, he was an easy touch. He couldn't comprehend greed.

Deacon Adams apprenticed his son to the commercial house headed by his friend Thomas Cushing, but after a few weeks Cushing was obliged to report that the lad just wouldn't do.

He then got a clerkship in the Boston market, municipally owned. His first political job, it paid but a pittance. He was twenty-four.

In 1748 Deacon Adams died. That same year Samuel, Jr., married Elizabeth Checkley, a minister's daughter, and they settled in the house in Purchase Street, which he had inherited. They had five children, only two of whom lived to be adults.

Samuel also inherited a brewery, a flourishing business, which he neglected until it was run to earth and sold over his head.

In 1753 he was made city scavenger. Still, his first interest never was in garbage; it was in district politics.

His wife died in 1757, and seven years later he married another Elizabeth, Elizabeth Wells. They had no children.

Samuel got a better job. He was made one of the six tax collectors of Suffolk County. He who never could take care of his own money was appointed to take care of that of others. He failed again. He was short in his accounts year after year, until the sum rose to almost £7,000, a fortune. He could not explain where it had gone.

Lieutenant Governor Hutchinson in later years liked to remind the public of these arrears, which were never fully made up or forgiven, and would speak and write of Adams' "defalcations." In truth, the man was palpably poor, and nobody who knew him thought for an instant that he had done anything dishonest. All five of the other tax collectors likewise were short, though none so much short as Samuel Adams.

That a business failure should steer the Ship of State was a fact to appall, but it did not faze Samuel Adams, and his public, a large one, still had confidence in him.

Even as a young man fresh out of college he had begun to make the town meeting his own.

Tacitus tells us that the ancient Germans used to debate every important question twice—once when they were drunk and again when they were sober. One time was enough for the old New Englanders; yet historians unhesitatingly tell us that the town meeting is directly derived from the Teutonic folkmote or -moot, from which, etymologists add, we get our expression "moot point," meaning a debatable point, one that should be taken up at the next moot.

The adult male residents of a given New England community, provided they owned some manner of property, would gather together at least once a year and talk and argue, fixing their own tax rate, arranging their own affairs. Since it was the way they wished to conduct themselves, and since they had no manner of aristocracy or hereditary rulers, this right was written into the royal charter granted to the province. Samuel Adams and the many who came to follow him were purists; they believed in the letter of the law, taking the charter *in toto*, literally.

Largely as a result of the Puritan revolution in England and later the so-called Glorious Revolution of 1688, the real power there had shifted from the Crown to Parliament, but the colonists had had nothing to do with this, and they insisted upon following their old ways. The New England town meeting too had changed, but this was a *permissible* change, since it was not specifically forbidden—as indeed it had not been anticipated—by the charter. The town meeting in Boston soon did much more than administer town affairs. It adopted resolutions on matters of international importance. It disapproved of Parliamentary actions. It arrogated unto itself powers never meant for it; and all the smaller town meetings throughout Massachusetts, and soon everywhere else in New England, did the same.

Samuel Adams came to be known as the Man of the Town Meeting. It was his métier. He corresponded with the leaders in smaller communities; he set in motion the machinery by means of which all sorts of special sessions could be called. Often he himself was the moderator of the meeting in Boston, or its secretary. In any event he and the fellow members of the Caucus clubs, having conferred in advance, knew exactly what they wanted; and usually they got it.

History was turning a page. The war with the French and the Indians, the first global war, was over. The peace treaty signed in 1763 gave Great Britain all of what had been French America, besides many other large land areas elsewhere in the world, and there was a huge money debt to be paid. The American mainland colonies, as distinct from the more amenable West Indian colonies, had been almost ignored by the mother country, which had treated them with "salutary neglect." That must be changed.

The statesmen of England in the 1760's and 1770's were not geniuses—they were not even very good statesmen—but they saw their duty, plain and clear, and they legislated accordingly.

CHAPTER THREE

Mr. Grenville Calls the Turn

There was no prime minister of Great Britain in the eighteenth century. The principal member of the cabinet sometimes was called the *first* minister, which of course came to the same thing, but the title as such did not exist.

"Where?" George Grenville cried in the House of Commons, as he spread his hands, *where* could he find a substitute for the proposed tax on cider, to which so many of the members were opposed? *Where?*

Grenville was always a bore. He was a man of figures. The war just ended, he reminded members, had left Great Britain with a national debt of £158,000,000, the largest in history. How was this debt to be paid, or even the interest of almost £5,000,000 a year? *Where* would he find taxes when the Commons had just voted to reduce the land tax from four shillings to three shillings an acre, and when the Commons was opposing his cherished tax on cider? *Where?*

At this point some irreverent person started to whistle a popular hymn of the period: "Oh, Gentle Shepherd, Tell Me Where." The members roared with laughter. Dry-as-dust Grenville thereafter would be known as the Gentle Shepherd.

The betting was that he would not last long, because the King simply couldn't stand him. Grenville's illustrious predecessor, William Pitt, had been bad enough. With his flashing eyes, his accipitrine beak, his florid complexion, Pitt was the man who had won the greatest war on record single-handedly, or at least so he believed, and he had been wont to address his sovereign in thunderous tones, the voice of Stentor. William Pitt, though he was adored in the American colonies, which named cities after him—Pittsburgh, Pennsylvania, for instance, and Pittsfield, Massachusetts—at home was a leader who led nobody. He did not have a program, and neither did he have a policy. What he did have was the ability to stun his hearers, snowing them under a drift of words. Members of the audience were breathless when this oratorical giant had finished speechifying, though it is not likely that many of them could have told you what it had all been about.

Pitt was magnificent. He was too much the lone wolf to be bothered by the practicalities of politics—committees and voting lists, promises, trivia like that. When he rose, a hush fell upon the chamber, for nobody knew, as he opened his mouth, what he was about to say. When he was finished, the applause would be heartfelt. Members would swear that they had never before been so moved. Those same members, however, then proceeded to vote the way they had been told by their nonoratorical leaders—or the way they had been bribed.

Pitt had planned everything about the war except how to pay for it. This chore was left to his brother-in-law, George Grenville.

Pitt had raged, intoxicated by his own verbosity. Grenville lectured, using monosyllables, which infuriated the King, who, though admittedly stupid, was not all *that* stupid.

The Gentle Shepherd lost his fight for a cider tax, but he was by no means discouraged, for he was convinced that the American colonies would do much to make up the deficit. He never had been to America, and neither had anybody else in the cabinet, but the colonies of late had appointed agents as representatives in London, and Grenville called them in.

The continental American colonies must be differentiated

from the British West Indian colonies, which were very well represented indeed in Parliament. In the West Indies most of the plantations were run by factors, who were either lawyers or crooks, often both, while the owners, made rich by slave labor, lolled at home in England. These owners were in a position to keep an eye on the control of their incomes. They were known collectively as the Sugar Aristocracy. They bought titles; they bought seats in the House of Commons; they bought votes. There never was any doubt about where they stood, or any question of their ability to fight off trade restrictions they did not like. It was in large part due to these men that the system of mercantilism lately had changed from the control of trade in the interest of national policy to the control of national policy in the interest of trade.

So highly were the West Indies esteemed in Whitehall that at the end of the war with France there were large numbers of Englishmen who urged the spurning of Canada, which after all was a frozen waste, in favor of that much smaller but richer French possession, the island of Guadeloupe. Canada won, to the disgust of many a practical merchant. Anybody in his right mind knew that one acre in the Indies was worth a hundred on the mainland of America.

The uneasy colonial agents then heard Mr. Grenville explain everything. He was thorough about it. He was explicit.

The American coastal colonies were in debt, granted, but not so deep in debt as was the mother country. The public indebtedness of all the American colonies put together was only about eighteen shillings a head, while that of the mother country was eighteen *pounds* a head, twenty times as much. The average American paid sixpence a year in taxes, the average Englishman twenty-five shillings, or *fifty* times as much. Was this fair? The agents made no reply.

The war had changed a great deal, Mr. Grenville went on. Previous to it, the civil and military establishments in the American coastal provinces had cost the home country

£70,000 a year. Now they cost £350,000. Comments? The agents said nothing.

The so-called Molasses Act of 1733 was about to expire, and Mr. Grenville proposed to renew it—with alterations. The original act regulated commerce between the American mainland colonies and the West Indies, and its most prominent clause, for which it had been named, provided a customs charge of sixpence a gallon on all molasses shipped to the mainland from any non-British Caribbean island. Mr. Grenville proposed to reduce this to threepence.

This might seem, at first, a curious way to raise money. But there was a trick. Mr. Grenville also proposed to *enforce* the act.

Carefully, slowly, ticking off each point, the Gentle Shepherd told the agents something that all of them knew anyway, namely that the Molasses Act as it stood was a dead letter. The British customs service in the American colonies was encrusted with corruption. It presently cost the government £8,000 to collect every £2,000 in customs duties in America, and that, gentlemen, obviously was not good business. Bribery was conventional, formal, expected. The top jobs, given to Englishmen, were sinecures. The men appointed never went to America, but sent deputies, who were paid, as a rule, about half of their own salary. Unable to live on this, the deputies accepted fees to look the other way. The thing had become a system. The standard price paid to a deputy collector was one-and-a-half-pence a gallon, and the government got nothing. Mr. Grenville proposed to command collectors to go to America, there to do their own work. He proposed to enlist the services of the Royal Navy in this project. He proposed to try violaters not in the provincial courts of common pleas, where they would have sympathetic juries, but in the admiralty courts, which had no juries at all.

The American merchants had feared this. For some time they had known that the Molasses Act was likely to be replaced, when it expired, by an act reducing the duty on that product, an act that at the same time would insist upon a full collection. What they had *hoped* was that the duty would be reduced to one-and-a-half-pence a gallon, so that it would be just as cheap to obey the law as to smuggle. At worst, they had thought, the home government might set the duty at twopence. Even that would have worked a hardship on the merchants of continental America. When their agents reported that Mr. Grenville proposed only to cut the duty to three-pence a gallon, they were dashed. They faced ruin.

Rum was the soul of the deal.

The English were by no means the harshest masters among imperialistic nations. The Dutch, the Danes, the French, the Spanish, all had laws at least as limiting, for it was the thought at the time that colonies existed only for the purpose of en-riching the mother country. The French, for example, would not permit their West Indian colonists to ship to France that heavy by-product of the sugarcane, molasses, for fear the stuff would be distilled into rum that could soon outsell the native Cognac brandy. So the planters in Martinique, Guadeloupe, and the other islands under the command of Paris peddled their molasses, at low prices, to visiting skippers from New York and Pennsylvania and especially from New England. This was illegal, but so was almost everything else. The *British* West Indian colonists, controlled by the vigilant Sugar Aris-tocracy, had a monopoly on the home market, and the Yankees could not afford their prices.

The French molasses, then, was taken to New England, where it was distilled into rum. Distilleries were everywhere, it seemed. There were forty in Boston alone, twenty-one in Hartford, eight in Newport.

Where did it all go?

Some stayed at home, to be poured down the throats of the lowly, the laborers. There was a popular belief that ardent spirits were needed to keep up the strength of men who toiled in the fields and in the shipyards and on the ropewalks. Rum was regularly supplied on the scene of the labor. Employers had no choice. Gin, a craze in England, did not please Americans. French brandy was much too expensive. Whiskey—that is, distilled grain—until recently confined to Scotland and Ireland, now was being used not only as a beverage but as currency in western Pennsylvania and the Appalachian region, but it played no part in the lives of those who lived along the coast.

Rum, however, was ubiquitous. It was sent west, to the frontier. The Indians would give anything for it. Most of all it was sent east and south to Africa. The chiefs and kings who serviced the barracoons along the Ivory Coast, the Gold Coast, and the Slave Coast loved rum.

This, then, roughly the Rhode Island-to-Dahomey run, was the first leg of what came to be called the Infamous Triangle. Liverpool was known as the slaving center of the Western World, and Newport often was called America's answer to Liverpool. Newport, however, had no corner on the trade in human flesh, for New England swarmed with slavers; they were not unknown, either, in New York or even in Philadelphia. The blacks taken aboard off the African coast customarily were paid for with rum. They were then carried over the horrible Middle Passage to the West Indies, where they were sold to the managers of plantations, who paid for them largely with molasses, which thereupon was taken to New England to be distilled into rum, which was sent to Africa for the purchase of even more slaves, who were sold in the West Indies for molasses, which was taken to New England to be distilled into rum, which was used for the purchase of more slaves, which . . .

Many a staid and sanctimonious New England family today owes its security to this trade.

The Molasses Act, renamed the Sugar Act, interfered with more than this basic trade. It stipulated as well that all lumber sent from the forest-covered American mainland to countries of continental Europe must thereafter be sent through English ports, where its seller would pay duty. That hurt. The act provided for a high duty too on the hitherto free wine from Madeira. This would mean that the Yankee shippers could no longer afford to handle Madeira, which they had been paying for with their barrel staves, so that another profitable business was knocked out.

Moreover, Mr. Grenville firmly informed the colonial agents that in about a year's time he would ask Parliament for additional legislation in the form of a stamp act for the colonies. He notified Parliament of this as well, when he put through the Sugar Act. He was studying the situation, he said. This stamp act would raise about £60,000 a year, or about one shilling an American, which certainly wasn't much. Nevertheless, if the agents, after consulting with their home governments, wished to get together and suggest some alternative tax plan, he, Mr. Grenville, would be glad to consider it. They had a whole year.

It *sounded* good, this offer; but Mr. Grenville was on safe ground when he made it. The American colonies never would get together on anything, he was sure. They never had. They squabbled incessantly. They had very little trade with one another, the interests of each being different from those of its neighbors, and they had no machinery for working in concert.

The Sugar Act of 1763 raised a storm of protest from the American merchants, who brought all possible pressure upon their creditors in England to have it modified. The Americans indeed were desperate. With their smuggling forbidden, their trade with the Madeiras strangled, their lumber business clobbered with new and costly restrictions, how could they make a living? They owed the English merchants £4 million, and they had no money. They could barter among themselves but not with the men in England. The law demanded that British balances be met with cash. Johannes, moidores, pistoles, Span-

ish dollars, and pistareens could be used, but only according to
their value in sterling.

The colonial agents came up with no acceptable substitute,
and at the end of the promised year Mr. Grenville, his figures
well in hand, put the Stamp Act through Parliament. He was
sure that there would be no trouble. He was mistaken.

CHAPTER FOUR

Boston Was a Talky Town

Samuel Adams seized his pen. He was at his best when he was writing.

A fanatic has been defined as one who can't change his mind and won't change the subject. Most fanatics, understandably, are dull. It was not so with Samuel Adams. He was so enwrapped in what he wrote that he enwrapped others.

Boston was a great port, a world port, in America second in population only to the sensational Philadelphia. Boston housed fewer than twenty thousand souls. Such a town would hardly be considered a city today, when it would be lucky if it had one newspaper that it could call its own, but in colonial times a multimillionaire's purse was not needed to start or to support a journal, and Boston at any given time had from six to twelve of them. They were all weeklies. They were argumentative and not very informative, because what news they did contain was stale before it knew print, having been thoroughly chewed in the coffeehouses and along the waterfront. Boston was a talky town.

Some of these journals were Tory, but most were Whig.

These designations meant little even in England, where the Whigs were men who held office while the Tories were country squires who came to town now and then to attend Parliament and to complain about taxes. The names had almost no ideological connotation there. In the American colonies the Tories preferred to be called Loyalists, the Whigs Patriots.

Samuel Adams wrote for all of the Whig publications. His favorite was the *Gazette*, published by Benjamin Edes and John Gill, "the Trumpeters of sedition," who ran a printing shop at Franklin Avenue and Court Street (then named Dorset Alley and Queen Street). Since they had little news and not many advertisements—the Whig papers of course got none of the "official" advertisements, the "legal" advertisements—the Boston journals depended for their appeal in part upon letters to the editor and editorials, in particular the leading editorial, or leader, which occupied most if not all of the front page. It was the leaders, no less, that Samuel Adams wrote. He signed them, but never with his own name, using rather, as was the custom, classical names. He was Valerius Poplicola or Vindex or Candidus or Determinatus. He had at least twenty such pen names, but his style was unmistakable, it was so *un*fancy, and when the *Gazette* came out every Monday afternoon, there was a crowd waiting for it.

Authors are funny people. Almost invariably they aspire to do some kind of writing for which they have not been proved capable. Thus, the successful novelist yearns to write a play, the successful playwright a novel, and just as Charlie Chaplin and many another funny man dreamed of playing Hamlet, just as Giuseppe Verdi would have given his right arm to be able to compose a good string quartet, so the scribbler longs for another field of scribbling, in which, he is convinced, his peculiar talents will at last show at their best. Samuel Adams was not so. He was not a "seized" author. He never waited for inspiration to strike. Writing was not his life, only one means to an end. It made no difference to him that he never saw his own name in print, that his paragraphs were to be promptly thrown away. One of his biographers has likened Samuel Adams' words to cannonballs that sink a ship. They tear through it and out the other side, and then they plop into the sea, to be lost forever. But the ship *does* go down.

He never affected a pietistic simplicity, but neither was he abstruse. The calkers and sawyers, as well as the clerks, could understand him. No cipher was needed, no code book.

He was always there. Palsied, prematurely gray, he was in poor health much of the time, but he never missed a meeting he was expected to attend, never sent excuses. He served on a great many committees. Ordinarily he was either the chairman or the secretary of each committee, but even if it happened that he was neither, he was often asked to frame the resolution or the statement with which the committee meant to give voice.

In politics everybody likes to have his say, and flowers of speech flourish like weeds. Since no single committee member would permit his own contribution to be erased or even trimmed, the result could be an appalling mess, and the only thing to do was to dump the whole business into Mr. Adams' lap. He could be expected to untangle a wordy knot that the other members had tied. *He* would bring something intelligible out of it somehow.

He was not paid for this work. "No man but a blockhead ever wrote except for money," declared the infallible Dr. Johnson; yet Samuel Adams could not be rated as a blockhead.

He could write anywhere, under almost any conditions; but when he was in company, which was most of his waking time, he preferred to argue or to listen, making mental notes. He did not customarily take pen in hand until after supper, after evening prayers, when he would retire to his study. Betsy, that admirable housekeeper, would go to bed early, but sometimes, she told friends, she would wake in the middle of the night, and listen, and hear nothing in all Boston save the quill of her husband, which scratched on and on. He never paused, this late worker. He never paced the floor or glared out of a

window. The words came smoothly, and smoothly he set
them down, satisfied with them, a happy man.

In the case of the new Sugar Act he hit the right note
promptly—and loudly. Writing the official instructions for the
four Boston members of the General Court, he asked:

> For if our trade may be taxed why not our lands? Why not the
> produce of our lands and every thing we possess or make use of?
> This we apprehend annihilates our charter right to govern and tax
> ourselves. It strikes at our British privileges, which as we have
> never forfeited them, we hold in common with our fellow subjects
> who are natives of Britain. If taxes are laid upon us in any shape
> without our having a legal representation where they are laid, are
> we not reduced from the character of free subjects to the miserable
> state of tributary slaves?

Other alert men had known the same thought, asking how if
Parliament were permitted to impose "interior" taxes upon the
colonies it could be prevented from effecting a complete take-
over. The colonies had never questioned the right of Parliament to regulate their trade. That was taken for granted. But
now Parliament was going further, and was preparing to impose an *inside* tax, the stamp tax. As Samuel Adams was prompt
to point out, where would they stop?

Protests came from all over—merchants' organizations, town
meetings, provincial legislatures. The royal governors did their
best to shush them, but they would not be denied.

The first *formal* protest, and the most startling, came from
Virginia, where on May 29, 1765, a bare quorum in the House
of Burgesses—only 39 of the 116 members—passed upon certain resolves read to them, one by one, by a wild-eyed young
hillbilly new to the chamber, Patrick Henry. These said, in
effect, that Parliament had no right to tax Virginia and that
Virginia would not pay. The resolves, seven in number, were
to be voted upon separately. They got hotter as they went
along. The first four squeaked through by small votes. The

fifth won by exactly one vote, 20–19, and Patrick Henry, seemingly fearful that the rest would be defeated, pocketed them. The House the very next day rescinded the fifth resolve, by far the strongest, but meanwhile copies of all seven had been sent to various newspapers and were published up and down the land, the public's impression being that all seven had been adopted.

There were those who said that when a law was on the books it should be enforced, and that was that.

There were those who took up the argument, advanced by sundry members of Parliament, that the Commons was not supposed to represent districts, areas, pieces of land, but rather trades, interests, classes of society. These members contended, then, that Americans had "virtual" representation, whatever that meant.

There were those who pointed out that after all only one Englishman out of ten *in England* had a vote, pocket boroughs, family-owned seats, being common. That might have been true, but it did not help the colonists. Some few suggested that a plan might be worked out by means of which the colonies *would* be represented in Parliament, but most Americans snorted at this possibility. Some New Englanders, like James Otis, Samuel Adams' titular boss, exclaimed, as did Adams, that even if they could be got there, Americans representing the colonies surely would be contaminated by the ungodly institutions of the English. What did the young lords learn at Oxford and Cambridge? Otis asked, and answered himself in town meeting with "nothing at all but Whoring, Smoking, and Drinking." As for members of Parliament, they were "a parcel of Button-makers, Pin-Makers. Horse Jockeys, Gamesters, Pensioners, pimps and Whore Masters."

There were, too, the ones who noted that the population of the American colonies was growing much faster than that of Great Britain. The mother country presently had 8,500,000 people and the colonies only 1,775,000, but it was estimated that the child would overtake the parent by 1810 (actually this did not happen until 1847). Samuel Adams dismissed this with a sniff. "When our liberty is gone, history and experience will teach us that an increase of inhabitants will be but an increase of slaves."

He liked to use that word "slave," one that would strike a chill to any stout American spine. Actually he owned a slave himself at this time, a Negro girl named Surry. Betsy had inherited her, and the laws of property and those of marriage being what they were, the maid was Samuel's to do with as he wished. He freed her, but she lived on in the house in Purchase Street for many years.

The coastal provinces, numbering thirteen, had almost as many forms of government. The freest were Connecticut and Rhode Island, which elected their own governors. Most were under royal charters of one sort or another. Two, Pennsylvania and Maryland, were family fiefs, the former belonging to the Penns, the other to the Calverts. The Quakers controlled Pennsylvania, though they were outnumbered. Catholics were allowed in Maryland, where the Church of England was established. Virginia, officially at least, was a part of the Church of England establishment. All of New England, excepting Rhode Island, which permitted almost any form of religious believers, including even Jews, was firmly Congregational. Some of the colonies were in more or less open warfare with others. Connecticut had sent militia to the Wyoming Valley in Pennsylvania, which it claimed, a claim Pennsylvania denied. New York and New Hampshire were quarreling over the ownership of what later came to be called Vermont. Virginia and Pennsylvania were ready to fly at one another's legal throats, each in assertion of its own right to Pittsburgh at the junction of the Allegheny and Monongahela rivers.

Massachusetts was headed by a governor and a lieutenant governor, each appointed by the King, though the colony paid their salaries. The governor was Francis Bernard, an Oxford man, who told a good story and was a talented amateur architect. His wife was a sister of Lord Barrington, and Bernard was angling for a baronetcy. They had eight children. Bernard was not a crook, nor was he an infatuated fool, but he was more interested in his own financial affairs than in the welfare of Massachusetts Bay, and his chief concern was to keep out of trouble. The job paid £1,100 a year.

The lieutenant governor was Thomas Hutchinson, a grave, conscientious man, a great-grandson of Anne Hutchinson, whom the Puritans had exiled for heresy. He was a fond father and a successful merchant. He was reserved, perhaps haughty, and not well liked. Men called him a cold fish.

Both Bernard and Hutchinson, though Tories, or "King's men," had been opposed to the passage of the Stamp Act, and had so written to friends in England. The American populace, though, believed that they favored the Stamp Act, and neither one of them would lower himself by announcing the truth.

The legislature, or General Court, consisted of two houses, a council of 28 members elected each year by the old council, and the Assembly. The governor could negative, or veto, up to 13 of the 28 elected to the council. The Assembly was made up of 112 to 116 members, elected by towns, and these towns, through the medium of their town meetings, would give each delegate his instructions before he went to Boston. They served for one year at a time. Boston had four members, the Boston Seat.

The governor could negative any act of the General Court, and he could summon it, adjourn it, dissolve it at will. He was also commander in chief of the provincial militia, whose officers he appointed. There was a Superior Court consisting of a chief justice and four associate justices, and these men ordinarily saw eye to eye with the governor, though they too were paid by the province.

The party to which Samuel Adams belonged, the so-called

Whig party, had long controlled the Assembly, and recently it had come into control of the council as well. This General Court, early in June of 1765, after the Virginia Burgesses had passed some of Patrick Henry's resolves *but before the news of this had reached Massachusetts,* passed in both houses a circulatory letter addressed to the provincial assemblies of all the other colonies proposing that a central congress be held in order to discuss the onrushing Stamp Act. The governor and lieutenant governor vehemently objected to this letter, which Samuel Adams had written, but the two houses passed it anyway—and with large majorities. What George Grenville had thought impossible was about to happen. The colonies were getting together.

CHAPTER FIVE

Sons of Fury

It would be wrong to attribute the nonimportation movement to Samuel Adams, though this has been done. He was not a merchant, and the movement in its beginnings at least was essentially mercantile. It did not even start in Boston, but in New York, whence it quickly spread to Boston and Philadelphia, Charleston, the lesser ports. Farmers and others who lived inland were given no choice. They had what they grew, but for all "boughten" objects they were dependent upon the traders along the coast.

Adams was among the first to embrace the plan wholeheartedly and to push it. He had always dreamed of the colonies as a Christian Sparta in a new Puritan Age, and had deplored the purchase of "British Frippery" such as would have horrified the Puritans Bradford, Winslow, and Winthrop. "Bless me!" he cried in the *Gazette*, "could our ancestors look out of their graves and see so many of *their own* sons, deck'd with the worst of *foreign superfluities*, the ornaments of the *whore of Babylon*, how would it break their sacred repose!" Besides, the movement fitted in with his political ideas, and he did everything he could, which was a great deal, to further it.

The meeting at which the plan was broached was held in a New York mercantile headquarters, the Long Room of Burns' Tavern, and it could fairly be called both spontaneous and informal, though it was to result in the formation of the New York Chamber of Commerce, the first such body in the land.

In the beginning the idea was only to gain agreements that there should not be imported from England any article not desperately needed in the colonies, at the same time writing to the English merchants a plea that they work for the moderation or even repeal of both the Sugar Act and the Stamp Act. Massachusetts, Connecticut, Rhode Island, New York, Pennsylvania, Virginia, and South Carolina already had sent instructions to their agents in England to work toward this end, and additionally Massachusetts, Rhode Island, New York, and Virginia had petitioned both King and Parliament for relief; but the businessmen of the American coastal cities believed that more than this was needed.

The thing soon became a patriotic cause. Daughters and wives took it up, also the nonmercantile males of the ports, crying, "Save your money and you can save your country." Frugality came into fashion. All things English were placed on a black list. The tailors of Newport volunteered to work for fourpence a yard less in American-made goods. Rags were assiduously saved, and tow and flax were sometimes substituted for them in making paper. All sorts of persons agreed, whether freely or as a result of pressure, to abstain from eating lamb and even mutton, so that American woolen manufacture could be built up. The students at Harvard, Yale, and New Jersey College (Princeton) voted to forgo their commencement gowns. The ladies held spinning bees, and civic organizations and civic-minded private individuals offered cash prizes for the best pieces of home-made serge, sagathy, and shalloon. The women served and even drank Hyperion tea, a decoction of the leaves of the common redroot, which was something like wild rosemary; it was bitter, but they pluckily avowed that it was better than the real thing.

The biggest change undoubtedly was in the matter of funerals.

Europe had gone mourning-mad. Funerals were glittering monstrosities, top-heavy with extravagance. There were professional keeners, enormous catafalques, wakes, days-long feasts, parades. The American colonists, simple folks, seemed to have resisted this pomp and ponderosity. The coffin was likely to be a plain pine one, if a coffin was used at all and not just a winding-sheet. There were no hearses except in the cities and for eminent persons, and they were mere carriages or wagons draped with crape. There were few undertakers. Members of the family or friends washed and laid out the corpse. The sexton of the church dug the grave and rang the passing-bell, and his fee was a trifle. Ground space itself, for members of the congregation, usually cost nothing. The sermon, whether in church or at the grave, had grown to be an accepted institution, but preachers came cheap. Sometimes the old English practice of tossing sprigs of evergreen into the open grave as symbols of immortality was followed in America, but nobody even thought of flowers. Hired mourners were unknown. Except for Dutch funerals in New York, prolonged feasting was not the rule. Where extravagance *did* rear its ugly head was in the drapes.

Heavy black cloth of English manufacture was to be in evidence everywhere at a funeral—windows, doors, in the church. Members of the immediate family had to dress entirely in black, and near relatives were expected to continue in this fashion for a year or more, and widows, unless they remarried, remained in weeds for the rest of their lives. Every mourner, though not paid, must be provided with a heavy black scarf and a pair of heavy black gloves. These gloves and scarves were not to be used a second time anywhere else. One thousand pairs of gloves were passed out at the Boston funeral of Governor Belcher's wife in 1736, but even a nonentity, even a pauper, had to be honored in death by at least a few pairs. Andrew Eliot, after he had been the pastor of the North Church, Boston, for thirty-two years, one day counted the funeral gloves that he had accumulated. There were 2,940 pairs.

Pins too were given away, and brooches, bracelets, and rings, especially rings, which came to be as important and as expensive a part of even a modest funeral as the gloves. This "funeral jewelry" was made in England, and tons of it were sent to the colonies every year. The pieces generally were of black enamel, and though sometimes a single ring might cost as much as a pound, like the gloves and scarves it could be worn only once.

The American merchants, to bolster their nonimportation agreements, had asked patriotic groups to agree to certain economies, one of the chief of these being the cutting down on mourning material. Thousands did sign such pledges or gave verbal promises to that effect.

The movement to boycott British goods was an unexpected success at first, especially in New York and New England. It faded for a little while, teetered, and seemed to die, but it picked up again, becoming stronger than ever. So long as it was controlled by the men in the countinghouses, men who had no interest in charter privileges or rights or ministerial limitations or the balance of power between Throne and Parliament, it positively flourished. What killed it in the end was the angry influx of patriotism. The Sons of Liberty killed it.

They were given their name by a French Huguenot from Ireland. Colonel Isaac Barré was a vehement man. He had served under Wolfe in Canada, where a musket ball had put out his left eye and smashed the upper part of his left cheekbone, leaving a hideous scar, which when he waxed angry throbbed a dark, direful red. There was something distinctly Satanic-looking about the man, who was a good friend of the American colonies, raging for their rights in the House of Commons.

Quite a different person, though in the same chamber, was Champagne Charlie Townshend, Thin, young, well connected, an epileptic, he was determinedly flippant and used derision as a drover might use his whip. He was said to be extremely funny, and he had won his nickname from the fact that he was often drunk while delivering his most hilarious speeches.

One day, in the course of the all-too-brief debate about the Stamp Act, Champagne Charlie asked: "And now will these Americans, children planted by our care, nourished by our indulgence until they are grown to a degree of strength and opulence, and protected by our arms, will they grudge to contribute their mite to relieve us from the heavy weight of that burden which we lie under?"

Colonel Barré was on his feet instantly.

"They planted by your care? No! Your oppressions planted 'em in America. They fled from your tyranny to a then uncultivated and unhospitable country—where they exposed themselves to almost all the hardships to which human nature is liable, and among others to the cruelties of a savage foe, the most subtle and I take upon me to say the most formidable of any people upon the face of God's earth. And yet, actuated by principles of true English liberty, they met all these hardships with pleasure, compared with those they suffered in their own country from the hands of those who should have been their friends.

"They nourished by *your* indulgence? They grew by your neglect of 'em. As soon as you began to care about them that care was exercised in sending persons to rule over 'em, in one department and another, who were perhaps the deputies of deputies to some member of this House—sent to spy out their liberty, to misrepresent their actions and to prey upon them; men whose behavior on many occasions has caused the blood of those Sons of Liberty to recoil within them; men promoted to the highest seats of justice, some, who to my knowledge were glad by going to a foreign country to escape being brought to the bar of justice of their own."

The speech made a notable impression. Friends of the colonies wrote back about it, and Americans were quick to pick up the phrase "Sons of Liberty," which too soon came to mean violence.

There was a Sons of Liberty organization in just about every seacoast town and county, though not all of them had that very name. Seldom indeed were they organized, with bylaws, with elected leaders. More often they were only mobs. But—they were *there*. The very fact that their members and even their captains remained anonymous made them the more terrible in the popular imagination.

Mobs were not new. English cities swarmed with them. Apprentices, discharged soldiers, the unemployed rioted as a matter of course. In England, however, the mobs came and went, and, terrible though their ravages were, when they had worn themselves out, they dissolved, disappeared, never to come back at the same place in the same form. What made mobs so greatly feared in America was their air of permanence.

In Boston there were two full-time gangs, the North Enders led by Samuel Swift, a Harvard man, class of '35, and a lawyer, who preferred to stay in the background, and the South Enders, who were headed by a burly cobbler named Ebenezer Macintosh. Macintosh was the more active. He was often called the Captain General of the Liberty Tree, and would noisily supervise the hoisting of effigies into that famed elm at the intersection of what are now Essex and Washington streets.

These groups occasionally clashed by accident, brushing one another, but they waged open war every November 5. This day is known in England as Guy Fawkes Day, and our word "guy," the noun, comes from the scarecrowlike dummies that were paraded through the streets, later to be dumped upon huge bonfires on the anniversary of the Gunpowder Plot of 1605, when those present chanted:

> "Please to remember the fifth of November,
> Gunpowder, Treason, and Plot."

In Boston it was an effigy of the Pope, not one of Fawkes, that was burned, and the burning was customarily preceded by a battle. Each gang had its own effigy, and after parading it through its own district, each made for the no-man's-land of King Street, near the Town House, where they clashed by prearrangement. These encounters could be very bloody, and residents and shopkeepers in the neighborhood boarded up their windows in advance.

The Sons of Liberty were sometimes called the Cudgel Boys, sometimes an accurate name. More often they used less hooliganish weapons, and a quiet word might be all that was needed.

What was euphemistically known as night soil often came into play. Any man who had a shop and who refused to heed the warning of the local Sons of Liberty might wake up one morning and find that his windows had been bedaubed with human feces. The stuff was readily obtained. Every house and shop had a privy, or jakes, in the backyard. The cleaning-off was unpleasant work, in the course of which the word would go around that so-and-so must be selling English goods, for the Sons of Liberty had paid him a visit. That, of course, was bad for business.

A commoner threat was that of tar-and-feathering.

Perhaps because feathers have always seemed frivolous, this colonial punishment has loomed before a later generation as something ludicrous, an act of clowning, a vulgar but harmless display of spirits. In truth there was nothing funny about it. The feathers were mere decoration and could be dispensed with. The tar it was that told the tale—a tale of unabashed brutality.

Pine tar ordinarily was used, a stickier, sharper substance than beech tar or the various kinds of coal tar. It was heated in front of the victim, so he might see in its sulfurous bubblings the pain that would soon be his—a matter that was significant. In Renaissance days it was the practice in most prisons to show a convicted man the instruments of torture, either one by one or all together, so that he might reflect upon them before the actual process began. He could, of course, change his mind. He could confess. Even as late as Elizabethan days in merrie England, when only one form of physical torture was permitted, the rack, and that only in certain circumstances and by order of certain high officials, the law itself insisted upon such a confrontation. The use of each wheel and crank and line and pulley was explained to the prisoner, so that he knew in advance just how he would feel when they were tearing him oh-so-slowly apart. Then he would be taken back to his cell to think it over.

The reason for this practice was the confession that might well expose a plot against the state or against the lives of certain statesmen. Torture was used only in treason cases.

No such pretense at justification existed in the colonial American tar-and-feathering. No confession was sought. The deed to be done was simple savagery.

The victim was stripped to the waist. A ladle with a long handle was used, and the hissing, spitting stuff was poured over his shoulders, his chest, his back. A little of it might be emptied upon the top of his head, which could cause him to be blinded permanently in one or both eyes. If his breeches and underpants had been ripped off, a ladleful might be dumped upon his genitals.

If the wretch was but to be dropped into a ditch for his friends to rescue later, then feathers were wasted upon him, but if he was to be mounted on a rail, one leg on each side, to be toted through the streets, the carriers jogging it furiously so that the fellow felt as though he were being split in half, *then* feathers—or, in the absence of feathers, ashes or ripped-up clothes—were copiously applied.

Getting the stuff off was the most painful part of the business. Skin would come with it, and days, even weeks, were needed to complete the job, though in a larger sense no victim of a tarring party ever did recover completely.

The practice was not common, and it seems to have been confined to the New England provinces at one end of the colonial line and the provinces of the Deep South, the Carolinas and Georgia, at the other. The middle provinces abstained.

The *threat*, however, was always there. A man who had made himself unpopular, for whatever reason, might have a ball of cold tar, encased in a fluff of feather tops, slipped into his hand in some public place or sent to him by messenger. He would understand. He would move away.

The case of John Mein illustrates the point. He was a stout-hearted Scot who moved to Massachusetts just after the French and Indian War and, in partnership with a man named Fleeming, ran a bookshop and weekly newspaper. Every bookseller ran a newspaper then. The Mein-Fleeming one was called the *Chronicle*. In addition—and this was his own enterprise—Mein started the first circulating library in Boston.

The *Chronicle* was kept neutral for several years, but at last Mein began to take the government's side. He was warned, but he snorted defiance. Samuel Adams himself publicly abjured him to cease "this opposition to an awakened, an enlightened, and determined continent," but he continued in the columns of the *Chronicle* to urge the merchants of Boston to break their nonimportation agreements. He was attacked on King Street near his office, which was wrecked. On October 28, 1769, some of the less responsible citizens, all unidentified, having given the tar treatment to a man accused of informing on a smuggler, paraded this rascal through the streets for three hours, and they were careful to stop him for a goodly while before the Mein and Fleeming office, giving John Mein a good look. Afterward Mr. Mein was handed the chunk of cold tar and the feathers. This, together with the attack, was enough for him. He left America on the next ship.

CHAPTER SIX

The Answer Was Brickbats

George III, a goggle-eyed, querulous soul, had been brought up to be a king, not a yes-man. George's grandfather and great-grandfather, Georges II and I, had ruled Great Britain in an offhand manner, being much more interested in their hereditary German state of Hanover. George I had not even taken the trouble to learn English, a language his son George II spoke with a decided accent.

George III, succeeding near the end of the Seven Years' War, was the first British-born monarch since Anne, and he was fond of reminding men of this fact. Doggedly he did whatever he could to make himself a real rather than an in-name-only sovereign. Through his political hatchet man, Lord Bute, he purchased Parliamentary votes, paying not in cash but in pensions and public offices. It looked alarmingly as though he hoped to bring back the prerogatives of the Stuarts. He frightened the Whigs at home, and he never did understand the American colonists. As a family man George III had a record that was not marked by a single redeeming vice; he made a fair but stern father, and he treated the colonists as though they were froward children.

Grenville had told the colonial agents that he was giving them a whole year in which they might think up a better system of raising money than the stamp tax. He had not given them a veto over the Stamp Act but only a warning that such an act would be forthcoming. He had tried to persuade them, in effect, to endorse the act unseen and unread; and they had quite properly refused to do this.

To the provincial legislatures, always mindful that the right to tax was the right to destroy, it looked as though Mr. Grenville were about to execute a coup that would crush them. He would trample upon their rights, rights that in most cases had been granted them by one English monarch and confirmed by two others. *Vivat rex!*

Champagne Charlie's complaint was not an uncommon one. Many Britons felt the same way. What the Devil *did* these colonials want? What right had they, the pampered darlings, to talk about charters?

As the terrible day, November 1, 1765, approached, the petitions and resolutions continued to flow in; the American newspapers and especially the Boston *Gazette* waxed increasingly shrill; liberty trees or liberty poles were dedicated or erected in virtually every town and village in the colonies.

The Gentle Shepherd was not perturbed. He predicted that there would be no trouble. He was sure of his statistics.

Nevertheless, Mr. Grenville took certain precautions. He had been told, for instance, that English agents and supervisors in America tended to be uppity, harsh, arrogant, and were in consequence not liked, so he was making every effort to get local men for the Stamp Act jobs. He had made it clear that the commissioners to be appointed must perform the work themselves and not through deputies, and he set their salaries at £300 a year, which was munificent.

These representatives were to be authorized to sell not the stamps themselves but stamped paper. This paper was made, of course, in England, and great shiploads of it were to be sent across the sea. It was to be used in virtually every legal transaction—leases, apprenticeships, sales, mortgages, ship clearances, land deeds, liquor licenses. It need not be used in criminal courts but must be used in all other courts. A shilling was to be paid on every pack of cards sold, and tenpence for every pair of dice. It would cost a young couple £2 to get married. It would cost a college graduate £2 to get his diploma, it already having cost him £2 to matriculate. Law students, even after they had passed their examinations, would have to pay £10 to be admitted to the bar, a tremendous sum (in England the corresponding fee was only £6) which would have ruled out such lawyers as the young John Adams, the young Patrick Henry.

It is notable that lawyers made up one of the three most articulate classes in colonial America, the other two being printer-publishers and tavern keepers, both of whom would be taxed also under the new law.

The stubbornness of the resistance to the Stamp Act, and its angriness, astonished everybody. The congress that had been called to meet in New York, very largely as a result of the work of Samuel Adams, proved, to the patriots at first, a disappointment. Adams himself, who had just been elected to the Boston Seat of the Assembly and had immediately taken over its leadership, was not a delegate to the Stamp Act Congress. The most conspicuous delegate from Massachusetts was the volcanic James Otis, but his day would appear to have passed, for he was a man who was horrified by the very mention of independence and who, for all his fiery oratory, was mixed in his motives, clinging still to the belief that equal representation for the colonies in the British Parliament could somehow be achieved. The congress debated for a long time, and came up only with another petition to Parliament and to the King, a petition that was not even looked at by either.

Another Massachusetts man, stout old Brigadier General Timothy Ruggles, presided over the congress, but afterward he refused to sign its findings, deeming them impertinent. The Massachusetts General Court, on a motion by Samuel Adams, censored him for this.

The only other delegate who refused to endorse the proceedings was Robert Ogden, who, as a reprimand, was removed from his post as speaker of the New Jersey House.

The radicals were coming into control. There was revolution in the air.

Some did not perceive this, and though they were opposed to the passage of the Stamp Act, they saw no reason why once it was a part of life they should not assist in the enforcement—at £300 a year. Richard Henry Lee of Virginia, one of the fathers of the independence movement, sometimes called the Cicero of America, put in for the job in his home province and, because he had powerful connections, almost got it. Then he realized that he was holding a hot potato and dropped it. So astute a political observer as Benjamin Franklin arranged while in England to get stamp distributorships for a couple of friends back home, Jared Ingersoll of Connecticut and John Hughes of Pennsylvania. They were both good men, and Franklin supposed that he was doing them a favor. What he did was ruin their careers. They were soiled by the Stamp Act pitch even before their authorizations arrived, and each was called upon by a large body of truncheon-bearing Sons of Liberty to resign, whereafter they became political exiles.

The Sons were activists. They reasoned that petitions and other pleas were never going to do any good, and that to seize and perhaps destroy the stamps themselves would not help; England would simply send over more. Therefore, the best thing to do was to call upon the distributors-designate and demand that they resign. This they did, all up and down the coast.

For a change, the Sugar Aristocracy was now working with the agents of the mainland colonies, for though the Sugar Act was designed to benefit them at the expense of the others, the Stamp Act would work a hardship on both. As a whole, however, the West Indies, like Nova Scotia, though they grumbled, did not actively oppose the Stamp Act. There were exceptions. On Nevis and St. Kitts the stamped paper was burned. A group of Patriots at New Providence, the Bahamas, dug a grave, placed beside it the man who had been appointed to sell the stamped paper, and told him that they would bury him alive if he did not quit. He quit. Bermuda, Antigua, Jamaica, Grenada, and Barbados, however, bowed to the law, as did Nova Scotia.

No colony was kind to the stamp-paper distributors, who were looked upon as personal enemies. Rhode Island, the home of the slavers, of privateers, and until lately of pirates, was notably violent, but it was Massachusetts, as all had expected, that led the way.

On the morning of August 14, 1765, Bostonians awoke to hear of and then hurry to view two figures hanging from the Liberty Tree. One represented a man, more or less, and there was a sign on it with the name OLIVER ANDREW.

Andrew Oliver was the secretary of the colony, in effect the number three man, and he was a brother-in-law of the lieutenant governor, Thomas Hutchinson, who also happened to be president of the Massachusetts council, judge of probate of Suffolk County, and chief justice of the provincial supreme court. Of more immediate importance was the fact that rumor had it—and had it correctly—that he, Oliver, was about to be appointed stamp distributor.

The other figure on the tree suggested a jackboot, with something that might have been meant to be a devil—at least it had horns—peeping out of it.

The boot was easily read, for often it had been used in England to represent Lord Bute, an amiable Scot who pronounced his title that way. The Earl of Bute was attached to the household of the dowager Princess of Wales, mother to the King. She had valued him at first because he played a good game of whist and later, according to report, because of other, more physical accomplishments. Bute, who might have been born for backstairs work, assuredly was the princess's principal political adviser, and George III had, as it were, inherited him in that capacity. He did the King's dirty work in Parliament. He was thought to be—though he wasn't at all—the chief framer of the Stamp Act.

Were the figures on the tree a schoolboy prank? There was nothing playful about the citizens who in silence viewed these dangling grotesqueries. They knew that the Sons of Liberty were serving notice.

Governor Francis Bernard was perturbed. He had long aspired to be a *popular* governor, but now he sniffed the beginnings of an insurrection, and he thought of retiring to the safety of Castle William on an island three miles out in the bay. Instead, he called a special meeting of the provincial council.

The lieutenant governor, that Pooh-Bah, no longer was worried about *his* lack of popularity. His standoffishness made him a natural target for the radical orators. He still thought that the Stamp Act was a mistake, and he meant to do whatever he could to cause that mistake to be corrected, but he would not stoop to justify himself in public. Recently he had seen plenty of evidence that he was not loved. Nevertheless, now, in his capacity as chief justice, he ordered the sheriff to cut down the effigies. There was no police department.

The sheriff, one Stephen Greenleaf, took a good look at the situation and reported back that it would be as much as his life and the lives of his deputies would be worth to touch those figures.

There the matter rested for a little while.

Toward sundown the still anonymous Sons of Liberty took down both effigies and carried them to Andrew Oliver's fine square white house on Fort Hill, a house that was reputed to contain, among other treasures, the largest looking-glass in North America. They smashed the little white picket fence and a few windows as well, calling for Oliver to come forth. This he could not do, for he had taken refuge in the home of a neighbor. The mob, momentarily frolicsome, "beheaded" the effigy of Oliver in Oliver's own front yard, and then, after many a jeer, they proceeded in a body to a wharf at the foot of Kilby Street.

Andrew Oliver owned this wharf. He had lately started to build a low, houselike structure upon it, meaning to make this into shops, an investment. However, the mob had heard that it was intended to be the stamp-paper distribution office, and so they took it apart. They carried the beams and boards to the top of Fort Hill, where they made a huge fire on which they tossed the effigies.

It was late, and this should have satisfied them. Indeed many did start for home, but others, the die-hards, went back to Oliver's house and started to break the windows that they had neglected to break on their earlier visit.

Governor Bernard, alarmed, sent word to the colonel in charge of the militia in that district to do something about chasing the men home. He ordered him at least to beat an alarm. The colonel replied that he had no drummers; they were all on Fort Hill.

After that the governor took refuge in Castle William.

Lieutenant Governor Hutchinson and Sheriff Greenleaf went to Secretary Oliver's house and made some attempt to quell the riot, but they were pelted with stones.

By this time most of the "respectable" members of the gathering had gone home. What remained were the roughest of the rough. These men broke into the house and reduced to splinters all the furniture they found, including the famous mirror. They had a wonderful time, too, in the wine cellar.

Next day Andrew Oliver, closely watched, stood in front of the Liberty Tree and assured a crowd that he did not want the distributorship, presumably on its way then, and that if he was forced to take it he would resign. There was not a man there whom he would have consented to wave to if he passed him in his carriage, but now he virtually pleaded with them.

A few days later, when his distributorship commission *did* come, he was forced to enact the whole scene again.

In less than a week the South Enders were at it once more, and this time they aimed at Thomas Hutchinson.

Hutchinson's was perhaps the handsomest house in town, a large square stone building in Spring Garden Road, surrounded by beautifully kept lawns. It was here that the lieutenant governor, in his spare time, was writing his half-finished history of the Massachusetts Bay colony, here that he kept his notes, accumulated over many years. It was here, too, that he was dining with his family the night of August 26 when news was brought that the mob was on its way.

Hutchinson chased the others out, servants and family alike. He was determined, he said, to protect his own property single-handed. His daughter returned a few minutes later, vowing that she would not leave him. If he wouldn't quit the house, she said, she would stay there by his side. She meant it. He left.

Flint-fisted Ebenezer Macintosh's "chickens" were well supplied with rocks and bricks, and they smashed all the windows in the front of the house first. Then they chopped down the fruit trees in the yard and trampled the flower beds. They broke the rest of the windows, side and back, upstairs and down. They axed open the doors and swarmed in, yammering.

They broke the furniture, the porcelain, the oil paintings. They did not burn Thomas Hutchinson's manuscript and notes for the third volume of his *History of the Province of Massachusetts-Bay*. Instead they gathered them by the armfuls and threw them outside into the rain and mud.

The silver they stole. There was not as much brandy and wine as there had been at the Oliver house, but what there was they drank or stole.

They ripped all doors off their hinges and knocked down partitions; they even tried to tear away the cupola with which the house was surmounted. The cupola proving too sturdy for them, they started to slash the slates off the roof itself.

Rain had not fazed them, but the dawn did. Such men have no fondness for daylight. They left the roof and scattered, each to his separate hole.

Soon after that Thomas Hutchinson was back, picking up what papers he could find.

Macintosh was arrested, or at any rate detained for a short while. The sheriff soon dismissed him, apologizing for the inconvenience. Nobody else was even questioned.

It had been a large-scale ravagement, and the town of Boston was properly ashamed of itself afterward. Not only the expected King's Friends organization but also the General Court itself adopted resolutions of condolence addressed to Thomas Hutchinson, and when the lieutenant governor put in a detailed bill for damages, the General Court approved it without debate and passed a law to pay it. The bill was for £3,194 17s 6d. A string was attached to the grant, however. It was stipulated that there must be no criminal action against the guilty parties, whoever they were. Governor Bernard hesitated to sign this, but he did so at last because he knew that otherwise his friend would never collect a penny. King George, three thousand miles away, did not feel like that. The King said that he was sorry for Mr. Hutchinson, who should certainly be paid, but he could not approve such a precedent. That made no difference. Hutchinson had been paid and had signed a receipt long before the King even heard of the affair.

After that a man was found who said that he was willing to take on the stamp-mastership, but he changed his mind when a committee from the Sons of Liberty called on him. No bones were broken.

And all of this happened more than two months before the Stamp Act was to go into effect.

CHAPTER SEVEN

The Thunderer Himself

Early in July of that year 1765 the Grenville cabinet was turned out. It was not done, as the prognosticators had predicted, because he lectured the King; the King had been brought up to endure boredom, no matter how painful. Nevertheless, the cabinet was let go for a personal reason, and it was a royal one.

The King had been ill. There was no touch of the madness that was to cloud the latter half of his life; this was a purely physical ailment. Yet it frightened the ministers, who suddenly realized that although the King himself was temporarily unable to rule, no provision had been made for a substitute, a regent. They at once proceeded to make such a provision. The King's mother, the Princess of Wales, was naturally proposed as one member of the board of regency, but Grenville voted against her. When the King recovered and heard about it, he was furious. He assumed that Grenville had acted as he did because he believed the stories that his mother was Lord Bute's mistress.

The King's Friends in Parliament numbered a little over fifty, all firmly bribed. They never did constitute a majority of the Commons, but they were a well-disciplined minority strong enough to overthrow an unpopular cabinet, and they sacked Grenville.

Finding a successor proved hard. The stupendous William Pitt still commanded a small coterie of followers, but as before, he would not consent to take over any government unless he could first write the rules. The King's own uncle, the burly Duke of Cumberland, sometimes called Billy the Butcher—because of the savagery with which he put down the Highland rising in favor of the Stuarts, 1746—went out to Pitt's country place to beg him to act, but he refused.

At last a group of the so-called Old Whigs was ushered in, headed by Charles Watson-Wentworth, second Marquis of Rockingham. It was not a strong group. Charles Townshend, who always had a sneer ready, called it a "lute-string ministry, fit only for the summer," a ministry that would fall at the first nip of autumn. He was wrong. The Rockingham cabinet lasted a whole year.

Grenville now was leader of the opposition, strong still, and obviously the first move of the new cabinet should be to discredit him, thus weakening his influence. The best way to do that would appear to let fly at the Stamp Act, Grenville's pet.

The butt was a big one, and arrow after arrow was driven into it. It was patent to the dullest observer that the Stamp Act was not going to work. The Sons of Liberty, though without any central direction, without any regular means of comparing notes, had displayed an amazing ability to work together, and all up and down the Atlantic coast the stamped papers had been sent back or else stashed away in some obscure spot where they could do no harm.

The day that had been fixed to usher in the act, November 1, 1765, had been heralded in the American colonies with the tolling of passing-bells and many a weepful sermon. Flags everywhere were at half-mast. In Portsmouth, Newport, Baltimore, and Wilmington, North Carolina, the Sons conducted mock funeral services for Liberty, and they did it solemnly, not playfully.

It seemed impossible that the act could be defied. Such defiance would tie up all business, all trade, all law. The colonies
met this crisis in various ways, but all were firm, and all
effective. For instance, in Rhode Island, which always had
been a scrappy little province, the elected governor simply
issued instructions that the Stamp Act should be ignored; and
this was done. The *royal* governors of course protested, but in
vain, for their salaries were paid by the provincial assemblies,
which were strongly anti-Stamp Act, and the governors did
not dare to splutter too loudly lest their salaries be withheld.

The biggest problem, it had been expected, would be that
of the movement of ships. Would the Royal Navy seize any
vessels that did not carry stamped clearance papers? It did not.
The officers were eager to get the promised prize money, but
Halifax, the nearest authorized port, was far off, and if the
admiralty courts there decided against a seizure, the officers
would lose not only their time but also damage money. They
decided to wait until the whole matter was clarified.

In most instances skippers who wished to sail were issued
unstamped clearance papers as usual, together with a document
that explained that stamped paper had not been available.
These, it proved, sufficed. Most of the mainland American
trade was with the British West Indies, especially while the
nonimportation movement was in operation. These colonies, always excepting the little Bahamas, had resignedly accepted the
Stamp Act, but they did not seize ships from mainland
colonies that sailed without stamps. The same attitude was to
be met with in Quebec and Nova Scotia and also in Florida,
which at the moment was British.

Very soon underwriters in all the mainland ports were
offering insurance against successful seizure, with the premium
fixed at only 2.5 percent. *There* was a figure that anybody
could understand.

This state of affairs made things no easier for the cabinet,
shaky at best, for if the Stamp Act should be withdrawn with-

out putting a strong substitute into its place—assuming that this
could be done—a great many members of Parliament, whether
Old Whigs or Pittites or Tories, would be seriously alarmed.
These men saw the colonies as thirteen curs that were most
heinously biting the hand that fed them. The whole English
system of government had been challenged, and such a challenge, sir, must be met.

Mr. Pitt himself intensified, if he did not clarify, this feeling
when unexpectedly he came up to London and addressed the
House of Commons. He was magnificent, as always.

"I rejoice that America has resisted! Three millions of
people so dead to all the feelings of liberty as voluntarily to
submit to be slaves, would have been fit instruments to make
slaves of the rest."

This disquieted many. It seemed to make the whole business
somehow legitimate; yet it said nothing about how Mr.
Pitt stood on the cabinet.

Mr. Pitt himself soon cleared up this point. He had no confidence in the cabinet as constituted under the Marquis of
Rockingham. He seemed to detect in it, he said, "traces of an
over-ruling influence," presumably meaning Lord Bute.

He had not liked, either, the previous cabinet. George
Grenville was seated nearby, and the Commoner turned to
him, lest there should be any misunderstanding, when he cried
that "every capital measure they have taken has been entirely
wrong!"

He had no plan for setting things right, nor would he consent to share in the responsibility of running the empire. But
he *did* believe that the Stamp Act should be repealed.

"At the same time," he decreed, "let the sovereign authority of this country over the colonies be asserted in as strong
terms as can be devised, and be made to extend to every point
of legislation whatsoever. That we may bind their trade, confine their manufactures, and exercise every power whatsoever,

except that of taking their money out of their pockets without their consent."

The speech solved nothing, and only made many of the M.P.'s wonder whether Mr. Pitt really did mean to applaud those riotous doings in America. It was delivered January 14, 1766, and three days later the principal ministers met informally at Rockingham's London home. With tender care they framed a repealer, keeping it as much as possible in Mr. Pitt's own words. They also drew up a declaratory act, as Mr. Pitt had suggested, proclaiming that despite the repealer Parliament remained supreme in the matter of legislation in all parts of the empire.

The thing had a bad sound. There had been a declaratory act over Ireland in 1719, but the circumstances were quite different in that case. Ireland had been a conquered country. America was nothing of the kind.

Mr. Pitt had ceased to be the Great Commoner, for he had accepted an earldom. He was Lord Chatham now. He stayed in a darkened room most of the time, far from London, and refused to receive visitors or to open his mail.

The Declaratory Act avowed that "the King's Majesty, by and with the advice and consent of the Lords spiritual and temporal and Commons of Great Britain in Parliament assembled, had, hath, and of right ought to have, full power and authority to make laws and statutes of sufficient force and validity to bind the colonies and people of America, subjects of the crown of Great Britain, in all cases whatsoever."

The attorney general, Charles Yorke, expressed general approval but thought that the end should read: "as well in cases of taxation as in all cases whatsoever." Rockingham demurred. He and his fellow ministers had been careful to keep the word "taxation" out of both the repealer and the Declaratory Act. Mr. Pitt in the January 14 speech had asserted Parliament's right to *legislate for* the colonies but had denied Parliament's right to *tax* them. This tended to confuse the members even more than had the colonial differentiation between "internal" and "external" taxation, a differentiation Mr. Pitt himself swept into the dustbin of his scorn.

There was a full-dress debate. The ministry produced forty colonial agents, English merchants, and visitors from America, and each spoke against the Stamp Act. It was the merchants who undoubtedly swung the deal. Times were hard, and the nonimportation movement in America and the resistance to the Stamp Act had paralyzed a large portion of the transatlantic trade.

Rockingham introduced the repealer and the Declaratory Act on February 3. On Saturday morning, February 22, by a vote of 267 to 167, the Stamp Act was repealed. The Declaratory Act was passed soon afterward.

CHAPTER EIGHT

A Barrier of Brine

Jubilation engulfed England. An outsider, thrust into Manchester, Bristol, London, any English city immediately after the repeal of the Stamp Act, would have supposed that some great victory in the field had just been won, another Blenheim, another Ramillies, or Quebec. Toughs cheered each carriage that passed. Total strangers greeted one another in the street and exchanged congratulations. Resolutions were passed by fervently loyal civic bodies. Now cotton and woolen manufacturies would be themselves again. Toilers in both cottage and factory, who had not had a smitch of work these many months, now were being rehired, and in droves. The mirth was especially to be noticed in the ports, where hundreds of sailors, who had been close to starvation, were suddenly offered berths.

Sober second thoughts, always unwelcome, took some time to intrude. Those members of Parliament who gave any thought to America at all began to wonder whether the capitulation had not been *too* complete, *too* unabashed. Even after the passage of the Declaratory Act, would not the colonists so exult in their victory that they would be tempted to demand more? The English merchants hoped not, but they feared the worst. They had worked hard to bring about the repeal, but if the Americans were about to resort again to tar-and-feathers and the tearing down of houses, then the

merchants' work would have been wasted and once more
hard times would knock with a bony knuckle at their door.
So much depended upon the attitude taken by these erratic,
unpredictable Americans!

The English merchants wrote to them. It was not a hit-or-
miss, sometime correspondence. It was a deliberate and carefully planned campaign. In measured epistles the Englishmen
implored their American cousins not to gloat over the seeming triumph, not to exasperate the authorities at Whitehall
with I-told-you-so's, but rather to call upon their colonial
legislatures to vote resolutions of thanks to Parliament and of
course to the King. The repealer had been carried, the English merchants wrote, not because of the violence in America
but in spite of it. The colonists had *them*, the merchants, to
thank. They had behaved badly, and only the swift action of
their creditors abroad had rescued them from the punishment
they deserved.

The colonial legislatures were in a mood to accept almost
anything, and they accepted this reprimand. Every one of the
thirteen formally and in most cases fulsomely thanked King
and Parliament.

The news of the repeal had reached Boston May 16. On
June 3, Samuel Adams in his capacity as clerk of the lower
house of the General Court answered a letter from Governor
Bernard in which the governor had deplored the "popular discontent" prevalent in town. Bernard had hinted that it was no
time for the executive and legislative departments to try to
reach an understanding so long as certain evidence still existed
of "private interests and resentments," meaning, though he did
not mention it, the wrecking of the Hutchinson house.

In reply Adams wrote:

May it please your Excellency,
The House of Representatives of this province, beg leave to return to your Excellency our congratulations upon the repeal of

the stamp act; a most interesting and happy event, which has diffused a general joy among all his Majesty's loyal and faithful subjects throughout this extensive continent.

This is a repeated and striking instance of our most gracious Sovereign's paternal regard for the happiness and welfare of all his subjects. We feel upon this occasion, the deepest sense of loyalty and gratitude. We are abundantly convinced that our legal and constitutional rights and liberties will always be safe under his propitious government. We esteem the relation we have ever stood in with Great Britain, the mother country, our happiness and security. We have reason to confide in the British Parliament, from this happy instance, that all his Majesty's faithful subjects, however remote, are the objects of their patronage and justice.

When we reflect on the difficulties under which this important business labored, and the causes from whence they arose, we are truly astonished that they have been surmounted; and we gratefully resent [appreciate] the noble and generous efforts of those illustrious patriots who have distinguished themselves in our cause. Indeed, when we look back upon the many dangers from which our country hath, even from its first settlement, been delivered, and the policy and power of those, who have to this day sought its ruin, we are sensibly struck with an admiration of Divine goodness and would religiously regard the arm which has so often shielded us.

Having thus genuflected in the direction of God and the Hanoverian, the clerk of the assembly demands to be told why the governor thinks that there is anything wrong in the attitude of the members of the General Court. *He* mentions the attack on the Hutchinson house, which was the work, he declares, of certain "evil minded persons," but he sharply insists that, though these unnamed persons went too far, it could not be said that their anger was unwarranted. "There may, sir, be a popular discontent upon good grounds. The people may sometimes have just reason to complain." He serves notice then, and stingingly, that the people will go right on demanding their king-given rights. "Permit us also to say, that [opposition to a *rapproachement* between the executive and legislative branches] will disappoint the expectations of his Majesty and Parliament in repealing the stamp act; for it is most reasonable in them to expect that the restoration of the colonies to domestic peace and tranquillity will be the happy effect of the establishment of their just rights and liberties."

He was not alone in holding this opinion. There was still much to do. Americans paid little or no attention to the Declaratory Act, which could be dismissed as a mere face-saving device, but such thinkers as John Dickinson in Pennsylvania and George Mason and Christopher Gadsden in the South warned their fellows that danger lurked in that piece of legislation, and especially its preamble, which did *not*, they pointed out, distinctly disclaim for Parliament the right to tax.

The repealer, in truth, so far from bridging the breach, had left the two sides farther apart than they had ever been.

Most Americans, however, went on thinking that they had scored a tremendous victory. Hadn't the mother country backed down? Their delight knew no bounds when in the early summer of 1766 the Rockingham cabinet at last collapsed, to be succeeded by one headed by Lord Chatham himself, the incomparable William Pitt.

This seemed to clinch their triumph, for was not Mr. Pitt a friend of America? Had he not, in speech after speech, pointed out the rights of the colonists? Had he not specifically declared that he rejoiced in their resistance to the Stamp Act? Here was a victory indeed! Not since the war had this giant been at the head of the state in Great Britain, where men now could expect stunning reforms.

But—the giant was spent. He no longer was a power in the land, for he never left home. He was moribund. He would not take command of the cabinet of which he was the titular head. He would not even sit with it. He remained mumbling in semidarkness.

In these unprecedented circumstances it was natural that the strongest and most opinionated member of the new group, who happened also to be the youngest, should take over in Chatham's name. And who would this be? It was none other than the new chancellor of the exchequer, "the spoilt child of the House of Commons," the Honorable Charles ("Champagne Charlie") Townshend.

Townshend blithely avowed that he had a plan that would solve everything. True, it would raise a mere £40,000 for the British treasury, but all of this would come from America, which would be left no excuse for objection. Once this plan had succeeded—and it *would* succeed, of course—everything else would follow, everything would fall into place. Champagne Charlie was sure of it.

The plan was in three parts: The legislature of New York would be suspended as a punishment for its failure to provide for the troops stationed in that province; the hands of the customs commissioners in America would be greatly strengthened and the hated writs of assistance formally legalized; impost duties would be placed on glass, white lead, red lead, painters' colors, paper, and tea. These last, surely "exterior" taxes, would form an opening wedge.

Townshend was convinced, correctly, that such repressive measures, measures calculated to show the American provinces their place, would be welcomed by most of his confreres. He was not silly, as he seemed, but he was shortsighted. He *knew* that most members of Parliament would approve the course he proposed to take. He *assumed* that the Americans would.

Townshend introduced the three measures, all part of one master plan, on May 13, 1767, and saw them passed. He bubbled and seethed with confidence. It couldn't fail, he said.

He thereupon died, so that he was never to know what a witches' brew he had mixed.

CHAPTER NINE

Portrait of a Comet

The pulpit was not what it used to be in New England. There had been a time when the preachers laid down the law in all matters, civil as well as ecclesiastic, a time when the church was also the town hall. *Sicut populus, sic sacerdos*, Isaiah tells us, and this means, more or less, "As with the people, with the priest."

The saying was true no longer. New England pastors assuredly did influence public opinion more widely and deeper than pastors anywhere else could have done, but they were no longer almighty. This worked to Samuel Adams' advantage, for he never had to look upon them as competitors, which would have pained him. He himself had studied divinity for a little while, because his mother wanted him to, just as, because of his father, he had read some law, but his proper milieu was the committee room, not the pulpit.

He had many friends among the clergy, a class for whom he entertained the liveliest respect. His first wife had been a minister's daughter. He hobnobbed habitually with Reverend Charles Chauncey of the First Church, Reverend Samuel Cooper of the Brattle Square Church, Reverend Jonathan Mayhew of the West Church, and Reverend John Lathrop of the Second Church, powerful men all, good men, good friends. Undoubtedly his views affected them, and he might have suggested a sermon topic now and then, but he would no more have interfered with their regular parish duties than he would have expected them to interfere with his activities at the Caucus Club.

A possible exception was Mayhew, a preacher who has been called the First Unitarian, and of whom it has been said that "more clearly than any other man in colonial New England he viewed the fight for 'private judgment' in religion and the fight for personal liberty in politics as one grand battle in which all patriots could join with a will." He bitterly opposed the Stamp Act and was a vigorous proponent of what he called colonial union, a getting together of the various provinces for the purpose of protecting their rights. Mayhew, however, died at the height of his powers, on July 9, 1766.

Oxenbridge Thacher, though not a cleric, was another spirited worker in opposition to the Stamp Act, and like Samuel Adams a leader of the radical party and a regular contributor to the Boston *Gazette*. He would have gone far in the movement, for he was a much more personable man than Adams, but he died in 1765. He was on his deathbed when the news was brought of the passage of Patrick Henry's resolves by the Virginia House of Burgesses. "They are *men!*" he cried, and those were almost his last words.

Either of these two, had he lived a little longer, might have thrust himself ahead of Samuel Adams as the political czar of Massachusetts, but in that case he would have found Adams working for him as diligently, as intelligently, as before. For the man was born to toil in the cause of independence. He could not have done otherwise.

If he was ambitious, he never permitted his ambition to show. Most men who rise to power do so by stepping, howsoever gingerly, upon the shoulders of their fellowmen. It was not like that with Samuel Adams. He appeared to have no sense of competition. He didn't recognize rivals, if he had any.

Young men, some of them of remarkable brilliance, who

might have been expected to outshine him, he welcomed into the political organization he controlled. He made room for them, introducing them, praising them. Dr. Joseph Warren, the patriotic physician who was to send Paul Revere on his historical ride to Concord (which he never reached), and who was to lay down his life on Breed's Hill; Josiah Quincy, who though cockeyed was a powerful force on the platform; Samuel Adams' own young cousin from Braintree—all of these the Machiavel of Chaos received with not a trace of jealousy.

He never did mind taking second place. He never tried to outglow a fellow worker.

He was not, originally, the number one politician of Massachusetts. That title went to James Otis, in whose mighty shadow Samuel Adams for some years was content to stay.

Otis was a comet. He approached with roars and spitting, emitting a shower of sparks; he passed in a blistering blast of heat, blinding all who were nearby; and he hurtled off into outer space, rocking wildly from side to side, and leaving behind him ribbons of acrid sulfurous smoke—and nothing else.

Otis was a lawyer, and the son of a lawyer. James Otis, Sr., of Marblehead had long ago been promised the chief justiceship of the supreme judicial court by former Governor Shirley, now living in retirement in Roxbury. Bernard had not seen fit to honor his predecessor's informal commitment—as indeed why should he?—but gave the coveted post instead to his lieutenant governor, Thomas Hutchinson, he who already held so many offices. That Hutchinson was not a member of the bar seemed to the Otises, father and son, to compound the indignity, for, being lawyers themselves, they inclined to the belief that they were some manner of special high priest to whom was given a secret knowledge not vouchsafed to or ever to be attained by laymen. Bernard did not see it that way. Thomas Hutchinson, a very well-read man, in fact made an extremely good chief justice.

James, Jr., *it was said,* opposed the Bernard-Hutchinson administration for the rest of his life exactly because of his father's disappointment. The estimate doesn't flatter the man. He was, after all, a sincere patriot, as his record shows.

Otis was emotional and he was vain. He was above all an orator, and his oratory was most effective when he sailed in troubled waters, where it would send out the fiercest spray.

He had first won fame in his fight against the writs of assistance, an early no-knock legal privilege by means of which customs officials could crash into a warehouse, or any other house, without a warrant, provided they had some reason to think that smuggled goods were there. Young Otis took the case as the representative of a handful of Boston merchants, but he soon made it his own. He inveighed against the writs—which for many years had been acceptable in the mother country—with an eloquence that soared as though on the wings of song, bringing him thunderous applause. He lost his case, but he had made a deep impression on his audience. A member of that audience was the boy John Adams, who was greatly moved. More than half a century later the man from Braintree was to recall the event in his memoirs. "On that day the baby independence was born," he wrote.

The ex-President had a good memory, for fifty years is a long time. Otis did indeed by his leadership of the radical cause do much to further the idea of independence, but he himself could not tolerate even the thought, for he was fanatically loyal to the Crown. Unlike Samuel Adams, who never ceased to harp on the independence string, James Otis abhorred it—and said so. The Virginia Resolutions he called "downright treasonous."

Otis did not invent the phrase "no taxation without representation," but he did more than any other man to popularize it. Like his fellow Demosthenes, Patrick Henry, he tended to ignore inconvenient facts and to base his whole argument on "natural rights."

Samuel Adams, a much clearer thinker, scorned the idea that any kind of American representation in Parliament could ever be effected. James Otis, however, believed it.

Samuel Adams was called the Man of the Town Meeting, because he arranged them, called them, enormously enlarged their scope, and with breath-snatching dexterity twisted them to serve his own purposes. He was usually the chairman, but he was never huzzahed. James Otis, on the other hand, was the *darling* of the town meeting. When he entered the hall, a compact, resolute figure, and looked around, the citizens would rise as one man, cheering.

He was spectacular, but woefully unsteady. He drank. Even when he was not standing on a platform, even when he was seated among friends, he would sometimes shake both fists and screech his dire conclusions—only to fall silent a moment later, forgetting what he had said.

It is not known whether he had been drinking when he went into the British Coffee House in King Street the night of September 4, 1769. He could have been. He never should have gone to the place, for feeling was running high in Boston just then, and the British Coffee House was a favorite hangout of those connected with the customs, to whom James Otis was the Devil incarnate.

When he ran into John Robinson, the commissioner, who also had a temper, it was only a matter of minutes before one would start swinging at the other. Which one did it first is not known, and it is not important. As in the case of all bar-room brawls, everybody present had a different explanation of how it started. What *was* important was that Robinson had his friends around him, while Otis was alone.

Otis never really did recover from his injuries. He sued for £3,000, and was awarded £2,000, which he refused to accept. Robinson, who meanwhile had gone back to England, was called upon only to pay court costs, doctors' bills, and £30 for each of his own three lawyers.

Otis was taken out into the country, where it was hoped that the quiet would help him to recover his senses. Several times he returned to Boston and might for a little while seem entirely sane, but soon there would be a relapse. He went through the motions of turning over his leadership to his second in command, Samuel Adams, but for five years Adams had been exercising it anyway.

Otis' end was a fitting one. Completely crazy, an old man now, on a summer night in 1783 he rushed out of the Andover house of a relative in which he had been staying. There was a thunderstorm in progress, and Otis shrieked as he ran around the grounds, waving his arms. A bolt of lightning hit him and killed him.

It took a stroke from Heaven, men were to say, to shut that famous mouth.

CHAPTER TEN

Englishness at Its Worst

It is hard, looking at this man today—this picture on the schoolroom wall, a forefather, stiff, unresponsive—it is hard to realize that Samuel Adams was a legend in his own time. Miracles were attributed to him. In medieval times he would have been hailed as a saint.

When the North Enders and the South Enders of Boston failed one Pope's Day to put on their traditional Donnybrook and instead marched amicably together in one parade, even making some attempt to keep in step, as though to show that they were all Sons of Liberty, his friends and enemies alike attributed this wondrous union to Samuel Adams. He might well have had something to do with it, but that is not the point; the point is that nobody questioned his ability to perform such an act of reconciliation. It was taken for granted.

Lieutenant Governor Hutchinson in 1765 might write to England about Adams that "there is not a greater incendiary in the King's dominion, or a man of greater malignity of heart . . . who less scruples any measure however criminal to accomplish his purpose." The man in the Boston street could not care less. As he saw it, Mr. Adams got things done, no matter how.

The misnamed Mutiny Act was an annual in the garden of Parliament. Each time it was passed it was extended only until the next session. That was because the English, who had always disliked and distrusted standing armies, needed assurance that this enactment was only temporary. Here was a fiction, but it continued.

The act provided, among other things, that when troops were stationed in any colony, that colony must provide living quarters for them, also "fuel, candles, vinegar, salt, and beer or cider." When the colonists howled in protest, the top-ranking army officers so amended it that troops could be quartered only in empty buildings. Even then the colonists grumbled. Had not the learned William Blackstone himself, the most prestigious lawyer of them all, specifically ruled that this portion of the Mutiny Act was in fact a taxation measure? When, in 1766, two companies of royal artillery in two ships on their way from Halifax to New York were driven, half wrecked, by a storm into Boston Harbor, their commanding officer of course demanded accommodations. The governor gladly complied, and so did the council, which was Tory then. But the Assembly said no.

It was a flat defiance of the home country and might have led to an earlier showdown between the two parties, but Great Britain decided not to press it. The soldiers were soon on their way again. But Bostonians hailed it as an American victory. Rather unexpectedly, for he had not at this time made his power evident, Samuel Adams was regarded as the hero of the affair.

New York was not so lucky. New York was the headquarters of Lieutenant General Thomas Gage, the commanding officer of all His Majesty's military forces in America. His men were scattered, but most of them were at headquarters. New York, therefore, was being made to do more than her share, and she balked. This was why Charles Townshend had caused Parliament to declare the New York legislature dissolved.

Could Parliament do that? Had it the power? The money was not much, but the principle emphatically was.

While the other provinces watched with bated breath, the

New York legislature wavered. Then, just before the October 1, 1767, deadline, it decided, by *one vote*, to comply with the demand.

Until that time only Pennsylvania, of the various colonies in which troops were stationed, had fully lived up to the provisioning provisions of the Mutiny Act. Pennsylvania was controlled by the Quakers, who—"pigeon-hearted wretches" and "puling, pusillanimous cowards" Samuel Adams called them—always tried to avoid a fight. The other colonies made separate appropriations for the troops through their own legislatures, seemingly ignoring the Mutiny Act, or else they only partly filled the bill as demanded, overfilling other parts of it. In either case they determinedly denied Parliament the right to force such a law upon them.

New York had tried to do something like that, but the stark fact remained that New York had capitulated. It was a blow to the colonial cause.

That cause was not going well. The Rockingham cabinet had reduced the tax on molasses to one penny a gallon, but even this the colonial merchants found objectionable. Business was bad in England—there was a postwar depression—but it was even worse in America. And English merchants and ministers alike were waxing impatient.

George Grenville, as head of the loyal opposition, was pushing for sterner measures in America.

After announcement of the Townshend duties, there was a reawakening of the nonimportation movement in America. Once again patriots foreswore lamb, went about in homespun, and drank a vile concoction that was supposed to represent tea. The drive against the funereal use of black crape was renewed. The members of the South Carolina legislature voted to discard their wigs, made in England.

A resolution adopted by town meeting at Abington, Massachusetts, in March of 1770, is typical:

Voted as the opinion of this town that the agreement of the merchants and traders of the Town of Boston relative to non-importation has a natural and righteous tendency to frustrate the scheme of the enemies of the constitution, and to render ineffectual the said unconstitutional and unrighteous acts, and is a superlative instance of self-denial and public virtue, which we hope will be handed down to posterity, even to the latest generation, to their immortal honor.

The colonies, at long last, were beginning to think of themselves as a country.

But the heart had gone out of nonimportation. The merchants, who had started it, were disgusted because the Sons of Liberty seemed to have taken it over for purely political purposes.

The day was saved by Wills Hill, the irascible Earl of Hillsborough.

Simply to accept the responsibility of governing a land three thousand miles away, a land never seen by the average Englishman and unimaginable to him, was in itself an act of arrogance, but the statesmen went further. They appointed nitwits to take over this work. The ineptitude in high places in London was almost beyond belief.

Lord Chatham, affronted, had lost patience with the colonists, and his "cabinet of all talents" at last blew itself to pieces because of its own undisciplined diversity. It was succeeded by an amorphous coterie under the *de jure* leadership of the dark, squinting Duke of Grafton and the *de facto* leadership of Lord North, the new Chancellor of the Exchequer. North was an affable, bulbous man, an adroit parliamentarian despite his habit of taking catnaps during debates. Popeyed and with a receding chin and a sleepy voice, he was distinctly a King's Man. "America must fear you before she can love you," he told the Commons. The seacoast colonies, seeking a villain and denied by inborn loyalty the figure of George III, soon began to regard Lord North as a veritable Devil, complete with horns and tail.

A cabinet post was created, that of Secretary of State of the Colonies, and *that*, exasperated Englishmen cried, surely should prove that the mother country took her maternity seriously. The first man to fill this post was Wills Hill, Earl of Hillsborough.

Hillsborough didn't know anything about America, and he was not very bright, but he came from a good family.

The United States should erect statues to Lord Hillsborough, for assuredly he was one of the fathers of the republic. The nation *might* have come into existence without him, but he helped.

Too often it had been shown that petitions and prayers to King George were a waste of paper. The Massachusetts General Court, however, having formed the habit, sent through its agent in England, currently Dennys DeBerdt, yet another plea for relief from taxes and trade regulations. Massachusetts did more. It authorized its secretary to frame a letter calling upon the legislatures of the other colonies to express themselves in a like manner.

The result was the Massachusetts Circular Letter, not one of Samuel Adams' masterpieces but a good solid piece of argument that was to prove effective in an unexpected manner.

It was not a revolutionary document. It contained the usual protestations of undeviating fealty to "the King our common head & Father" as well as to Parliament, which it acknowledged to be "the supreme legislative Power over the whole Empire." It commanded nothing, but only called, hopefully, for some manner of customs reform. It suggested tax relief. It deplored the beginning of a movement to have provincial governors and judges paid by the Crown rather than by their own separate legislatures. It was a let's-get-together letter, and nothing more.

At first it caused little stir. New Jersey, Virginia, Maryland,

Connecticut, Rhode Island, and South Carolina promptly endorsed it, but the other colonies did not seem interested, and Pennsylvania, a pivotal place, was well on its way to tabling the thing without comment—when the storm broke.

Lord Hillsborough thought that the Circular Letter was impertinent, perhaps even treasonous. Just inducted into the new office—this was April of 1768—he was firm in his resolution that the colonies should be put in their place and kept there. He wrote to each of the governors instructing him to tell his legislature to ignore the Circular Letter, and he ordered Governor Bernard of Massachusetts to instruct *his* legislature to withdraw it.

Conciliation this was not, and the various colonies regarded it rather as a slap in the face, Englishness at its worst. The colonies that had not already endorsed the letter hastened to do so, even Pennsylvania with its Quakers. In Virginia—and he was only one of many—George Mason wrote a dignified but firm answer to the Hillsborough "squelch."

In Massachusetts Governor Bernard obeyed his boss by calling upon the Assembly to repudiate the Circular Letter. The Assembly did no such thing. It had recently, on the initiative of James Otis, constructed a balcony in its meeting hall, inviting the public to attend, which was something new, so that its sessions had come to resemble the crowded town meetings of Boston. When it gathered to consider the governor's letter, the feeling was so strong that even the governor himself sensed it, and before the Assembly could act he sent a message adjourning that body. However, the messenger never got to the place where the public was welcome. The door was locked against him, and the key was in Samuel Adams' pocket.

The vote to refuse to repudiate the Circular Letter was 92 to 17. The seventeen nay-sayers were not permitted to forget that vote. Not one of them was ever elected to public office again.

CHAPTER ELEVEN

The Coming of the Magnificent Brutes

There was much to be said about the British Army, both for and against.

In the first place, it was resented. The English still thought of an army as a temporary thing, a body of men assembled in order to meet an emergency. They had seen Oliver Cromwell's Roundheads take over their country, and Scotland as well, harshly repressing whatever their leaders looked upon as idolatrous, and making matters bleak and bitter all around. These monsters seemingly had appeared from nowhere, and Englishmen would not soon forget them. The very idea of a uniformed, standing army, a permanent force, was abhorrent.

Soldiers were dressed differently from their fellowmen; they talked a different language, lived in different places, obeyed different rules. A soldier in the late eighteenth century was no more a part of the human race than is, today, a prisoner in a penitentiary.

The British soldier even had a generic name, rather than one of his own. Just as the British sailor was known as John or Johnny Tar, so the soldier was called, in reference to the color of his coat, Thomas Lobster, which soon was to be shortened to Tommy. (The "Atkins" came later, when the army started to issue to all recruits manuals in which were to be entered name, age, rank, date of enlistment, length of service, wounds, medals, citations, etc. With each manual came a specimen form showing how it should be made out. On this specimen form was the hypothetical name Thomas Atkins. But the recruit had been Tommy before that anyway.)

Few British soldiers were English. After the Scottish uprising of 1745 under Charles Edward Stuart it was thought that the thousands of stranded, leaderless, and, in effect, outlawed Highlanders, men of rugged constitution and unquenchable courage, men moreover accustomed to obeying orders, might prove to be good soldiers. Such was the case. However, only a few Highland regiments still existed in the 1760's. The overwhelming majority of the rank and file were Irish.

What Englishmen there were in the ranks were hardly admirable examples. Many had been plucked from jails, and although impressment is generally associated with the Royal Navy, the Army practiced it as well. Men were fished out of gutters, or hit on the head in malodorous dives, to have a King's shilling stuffed into their pocket while they were still unconscious. Afterward, a hanger-on at the recruiting station would solemnly testify that the man had accepted this coin voluntarily. There were many such hangers-on. Some men did it for a living.

The word "impressment" has nothing to do with pressing a pair of pants or pressing toward the enemy. It came from an old French word, *preste*, or "ready"—the modern *prêt*—and meant that the coin the recruit accepted in advance of his pay from an enlisting agent showed that he was "ready" to serve his king in a military capacity. In Great Britain that coin was invariably a shilling piece, and its symbolism was taken literally, so that a great deal of importance was attached to the actual placing of the coin in the palm of the recruit. Once he had taken the King's shilling, he was subject to everything that the army or navy could inflict upon him. There was no retreat from this position, and desertion meant death. The fact that the poor wretch might have been unconscious at the time the money changed hands had nothing to do with it.

The term "cannon fodder" was first applied to German peasants, but it might as well have been meant for British soldiers, who were taught to walk rigidly erect toward the enemy, shoulder to shoulder, even while they were under fire. In the same way they were to stand motionless as the enemy ran shrieking toward them—without ducking, wincing, or firing until the order to fire was given. This, which was certainly *magnifique*, in the eighteenth century was also considered *la guerre*, and nobody did it as well as the British. It had worked at Quebec, a conventional battle, but though it was to result in hideous slaughter at Ticonderoga, at Bunker Hill, and at New Orleans and other fields, the army persisted in it as a thing inherently and splendidly British.

The redcoats were brutes because they were brutalized, but they were first-class fighting men.

Americans had inherited the militia system, whereby every able-bodied man of a reasonable age was obliged to do some manner of soldierly duty now and then. Companies were organized by towns, and were much like the later volunteer fire companies were to be—clubby and informal. Such a company might meet three or four or five times a year, to have their muskets checked, to elect their officers, and to drill while their womenfolk watched. Nobody knew much about the manual of arms—"the discipline," it was called—and the drills were hardly smart. Afterward the whole company would repair to a tavern. There were no uniforms, no regimental colors, no insignia, no banners.

These two systems met, not very happily, at the time of the French and Indian War, when the mother country sent large bodies of regular troops to America with orders to fill out their ranks with local volunteers or with members of the militia. The Americans gawked at the newcomers—at their sashes and guidons, their bugles and drums and fifes, their epaulets, their gorgets, their swords, their spontoons. Everything was so crisp and clear-cut! The regulars, of course, sneered at these dazzled dolts, and that was how the song "Yankee Doodle" was born.

The colonials made good scouts, but as infantrymen they were ridiculous. The British looked upon them, quite simply, as clowns. The only kind of fighting they knew was Indian fighting. The Indian fighter always got *behind* something, and any real soldier regarded that as cowardice. Of one thing the British officers were certain, and they were to spread their certainty when they got home: These clods, no matter what the provocation, would never *fight*. It was a mistake that, in effect, became an official military attitude.

The *Liberty* incident is often given as the reason why Lord Hillsborough at last ordered General Gage to send four regiments to Boston. In fact, though the incident happened at about the same time that the order was issued, Lord Hillsborough, communications being what they were, was not to hear about it for more than a month.

There was nothing special about the *Liberty* business, except that it was more than usually brazen. She was a sloop, and belonged to John Hancock. Fresh in from the West Indies, she took aboard at Boston the usual customs agent, who, however, showed a highly *un*usual tendency to do his job. Accordingly he was locked below. Hours later, when he was released, the *Liberty* was seen to be riding very high in the water and her declarable cargo turned out to be tiny.

The whole business was too flagrant to be ignored, and it led to a long and disagreeable lawsuit. The customs officials, many times threatened, more than once roughed up, believed that their very lives were in danger, and they took refuge in Castle William. Lord Hillsborough did not know about this when he issued the fateful order. However, he knew enough.

The colonists were not surprised by his move, but they

were flurried. For some time there had been a swirl of rumors about invasion. There had also been a report—well founded, as it happened—that the British ministry was thinking of invoking an almost forgotten and never enforced statute of Henry VIII in order to seize the chief dissidents and send them to England for trial. Nobody questioned this, and the only doubt concerning it was whether there would be one or two such prisoners. If two, then who would be the second—James Otis, Thomas Cushing, Josiah Quincy, Dr. Warren, John Hancock, Joseph Hawley? Nobody for an instant doubted who the *first* one would be. Samuel Adams, of course.

As it happened, this law never was invoked, but Boston was in a ferment just the same. When the General Court refused to rescind the Circular Letter, Governor Bernard had dissolved it, so now the legislative body, legally, did not exist.

Francis Bernard was recalled to England, ostensibly for a conference, actually to get his long-hoped-for baronetcy, and Thomas Hutchinson became acting governor. Hutchinson was particularly pricked by the Boston town meeting. Massachusetts, like all of the other colonies, had property qualifications for voting, but they were liberal and were not strictly enforced. Boston at this time had about 1,500 qualified voters, yet town meetings attended by 3,000 and even 4,000 were not unknown. Often the crowd was too big for Faneuil Hall, and the meeting was moved to the Old South Church. Hutchinson complained to Lord Hillsborough that "there is scarce ever any inquiry, and anything with the appearance of a man is admitted without scrutiny." Now Samuel Adams was going a step further. He had invited the town meetings of Roxbury, Dorchester, Brookline, Cambridge, and Charlestown to attend the Boston town meeting and to vote.

This consolidation body seethed. With Adams in the chair, it adopted all sorts of fire-breathing resolutions. There was talk of fighting the invaders to the last drop of American blood. A barrel of turpentine had been hoisted upon the gallows atop

Beacon Hill, the highest of the three hills of Boston, and it was understood, and indeed shouted in public, that at the first sight of the enemy the turpentine would be set afire, calling all patriots.

Nothing of the sort happened. The transports heaved into sight on September 28, 1768, and they were preceded by long-boats carrying officers, who conferred briefly with the captains of the four naval vessels in port. These vessels were reanchored with springs on their cables, each presenting a broadside to the town, each with its guns run out. They could have blown Boston to bits in less than an hour.

The 14th Foot and the 29th Foot and also a company of the Royal Artillery with five guns came ashore neatly and promptly with every bayonet in place, every button gleaming. Some of the men camped right there on the Common, while others, denied shelter in the town, and lacking tents, were temporarily housed in public buildings.

No shot was fired; not even a stone was thrown. A few days later the barrel of turpentine disappeared from Beacon Hill.

CHAPTER TWELVE

Light a Powder Train

The redcoats and the people of Boston faced one another, and they did not like what they saw.

It might seem that two regiments of infantry, not to count the artillery company, would be enough to keep a town in subjection; but this was not so, for several reasons.

A regiment then consisted, on paper, of six hundred men—officers, noncommissioned officers, and rank and file. Few regiments, if any, were ever up to full strength. Desertion always had to be dealt with, and despite the strict rules against malingering, there was sure to be some sickness. Some of the men were musicians, mandatory. Some were clerks, who counted as soldiers: an eighteenth-century British Army regiment was an organization of almost unbelievable complexity, especially in the pay department, and there was a great deal of paper work. Finally, there were fictitious soldiers, mere names carried on the regimental roster, whose pay went into a welfare fund.

All in all, any colonel who at a given time could count on four hundred able-bodied men could consider himself very lucky indeed. Three hundred probably was nearer the average.

It must be remembered, too, that Boston was looked upon by the British primarily as a capital, and at no time was the hinterland forgotten. Eastern Massachusetts was the most thickly settled part of mainland North America. The British must have had spies—General Gage controlled a slush fund designed for this very purpose—who must have reported a great stirring in militia circles far back from the seacoast, a significant reexamination of muskets, and everywhere the reissuance of powder and lead.

True, two other regiments of foot, the 64th and the 65th, soon appeared in Boston Bay, having come from Ireland, but they did not stay long. The 29th and the 14th were esteemed strong enough, and the others were sent off to Halifax.

The 14th and the 29th could not be called crack regiments —they weren't Guards—but they were good ones, respected ones, and not latecomers. The 29th, the one that tented on the Common, had been with Marlborough at Ramillies, and was to act with Wellington on the Peninsula. The other had served under William of Orange in Flanders, and was later to form one of the squares at Waterloo.

General Gage, a gentleman, had spent most of his life among the Americans. He liked them. He was married to one, a New Jersey girl. His orders undoubtedly were that every effort should be made to placate the inhabitants of Boston, and to avoid all incidents. He stayed on a few days in Boston, then went back to his headquarters in New York, leaving Lieutenant Colonel William Dalrymple, a nobly born Scot, in charge. There was no colonel. There never was. The colonels did not take the field but stayed home and drew their salaries. Their posts were political. The lieutenant colonels did all the work.

His men called Dalrymple "Steel Breeches," and they liked him. He was a good soldier, not a foul-mouthed, narrow-minded, damn-your-eyes martinet, but a man of sense and sensibility.

The 14th soon was installed in Faneuil Hall, in the very center of Boston, where the town's four hundred muskets were stocked. There had been no trouble.

A few naval vessels were always anchored in Boston Bay

these days, most of them sloops, though occasionally there would be a full-fledged ship-of-the-line like *Romney*, which had watched over the landing, and still held in durance, John Hancock's *Liberty*. Yet this show of force did not help the Army in its principal difficulty, that of keeping peace with the Bostonians. If the Army watched its men with excruciating exactitude, for fear of desertion, the Navy simply would not let its men go ashore at all. If life in the Army was hell, life in the Navy was more of the same and multiplied.

Indeed, desertion, and not irate farmers with pitchforks, was the most powerful foe that the invaders faced. Between thirty and forty redcoats vanished in the first two weeks, a loss this peace-keeping force, which could not count on large numbers of enlistments in America, simply couldn't afford. Most of them were recovered, to be savagely and publicly lashed, as was the custom, and one, Private Ames, was shot just two weeks after the troops had landed. But still they fled.

There was no large-scale movement to break from the military Moloch, no hint of mutiny. They deserted singly or in pairs, most often singly, but never in a group. They were always welcomed on the civilian side. Even those who did not need them, or perhaps did not like them personally and even feared them, were ready to harbor them and pass them along into the interior, because they knew this action would hurt the invaders. It is notable that though many deserters were forcibly snatched back, none was ever betrayed. The redcoats no longer were "our soldiers," as they had been during the French and Indian War, but "their soldiers."

Boston was a peninsula, what the French call a *presqu'île*, or almost-island. What with the Charles River, Back Bay (which *was* a bay then), and the harbor itself, it was surrounded by water—water incessantly patrolled by Royal Navy small craft—excepting for the Neck, a narrow strip of land on the south side. It was a matter of the simplest military precaution that the British should fortify the Neck, or at least establish a checkpoint there. The British were still thinking of those angry farmers, and they feared that arms and ammunition might be smuggled into town to promote an uprising. The Bostonians didn't like it. It made them feel—*hemmed-in.*

Ever since the Plymouth Rock landing there had been changes in the minds of the men of Massachusetts. No longer were they Brownists or Separatists, and few could be classed with Samuel Adams as Puritans. Yet their reverence for the Decalogue remained firm, and no commandment did they obey with more ardor than the Fourth.

It was wrong, yes, to lie, or to kill, or to bow down before graven images, and assuredly it was wrong to covet thy neighbor's wife or his ox or his ass, but most wrong of all, the sin that was the swiftest to be punished, was to take a walk on the Lord's Day. Some things could conceivably be forgiven; this, never.

Flogging was not new to the Bostonians, who, however, never before had known it to be done on such a large scale and so viciously, without prayers too. It was only natural that the Army floggings should take place on the Common, so that all could see the shredded flesh and hear the screams of pain, but that it should be done on the Lord's Day horrified the townspeople.

The officers did worse. They staged horse races in public, once again on the Lord's Day, and they made bets on them, passing the money back and forth right in front of everybody. The Bostonians complained to Major General Alexander Mackay, the officer in charge of the 64th and 65th, who paid a passing-through visit in May of 1769, and Mackay ordered that the races be discontinued.

Even a major general, however, could not call a halt to the seemingly harmless Sunday walks in which the enlisted men indulged. These strollers frequently stopped in front of some church in which Bostonians were praising God, and there they would sing. Their singing was not very good, but it was loud. Pious people spent a large part of every Sabbath in church, and they resented the choristers, whose favorite song was "Yankee Doodle." It, moreover, was mild. Most of the songs they sang were dirty, and some were even blasphemous, so that these aliens were breaking the Third as well as the Fourth Commandment.

The "convention" at Faneuil Hall, before it so ignominiously fizzled out at the approach of the transports, had been much concerned with "preparedness"—the checking of militia lists, the increase of drills, the distribution of ammunition, the building up of stores of food. All of this, it was explained, was in preparation for a possible war with France, though everybody knew that there was no chance of such a war. The convention had appointed a "preparedness" committee, of which Samuel Adams was the chairman.

Now, with the streets aswarm with enemy soldiers, any act along those lines would be put down as rebellion. Adams, then, must turn to something else.

Readers of the *Gazette* already knew how he felt about the English:

When I consider the corruption of Great Britain,—their load of debt,—their intestine divisions, tumults, and riots,—their scarcity of provisions,—and the Contempt in which they are held by the nations about them; and when I consider, on the other Hand, the State of the American Colonies with Regard to the various Climates, Soils, Produce, rapid Population, joined to the virtue of the inhabitants,—I cannot but think that the Conduct of Old England towards us may be permitted by Divine Wisdom, and ordained by the unsearchable providence of the Almighty, for hastening a period dreadful to Great Britain.

Bostonians, anyway, knew what to think of the redcoats. They had them in their own front yard. They saw and heard them every day. What was needed was to impress upon the adjoining New England colonies, and perhaps the middle colonies as well, and even those of the South, the agony that Boston endured.

Private letters were not enough. The aid of a united press was needed.

So Samuel Adams, at forty-seven, invented the news agency. He had some help from William Cooper and the printer Benjamin Edes, perhaps from a few others as well, but the idea was his. He did not slow his flow of letters to the local press. The *Journal of Occurrences*, or *Journal of Events*, or *Journal of Happenings*, was just a little extra work to be done late at night in the untidy small study in Purchase Street while Betsy slept.

It was in the form of a diary written by an always unnamed resident of Boston, and it went out every week by the regular post riders, free to the New London *Gazette*, the New York *Journal*, the Pennsylvania *Journal*, the Maryland *Gazette*, the Virginia *Gazette*, and the South Carolina *Gazette*. Many others would be sure to copy it.

Adams wrote the diary for almost a year, never missing a week, from September 28, 1768, to August 1, 1769. It was a great success.

Some attempt was made in nearly every number to give an account of civic affairs, but by far the greatest part of the sheet was covered with accounts of how the visiting infantrymen behaved.

A journalist then was not expected to adhere faithfully to the facts, but few could have gone as far astray as did Samuel Adams. An outsider reading his reports would suppose that Boston was undergoing a veritable Reign of Terror. Poor little Boston! Brave Boston! She might well need the assistance of those faraway places.

The redcoats here were acting not as an army of occupation but rather as a police force. Officers and sergeants alike had hammered it into the men that they could not use their weapons even as a threat without first getting the permission of a magistrate. A redcoat who was in any sort of trouble would be hauled before a civilian magistrate, and everybody knew how the magistrates would find, for the Sons of Liberty were still there, in the shadows now but fingering their blackjacks all the same.

Adams' friends were to contend that his stories were founded upon real happenings. If that was so, then the principals involved never would have recognized themselves. Did a lobsterback stub his toe and curse the pain under his breath? In Adams' stories it became a tirade, full of blasphemy and vituperation. Did one of them slip and inadvertently bump a passerby with his shoulder? That became a bloody and unprovoked attack.

Adams, who ordinarily avoided such a subject, was especially lurid in the *Journal* when he described sexual assaults, which it turned out were happening every day all over town. He bore down on this subject, sparing no detail.

Most of the lobsterbacks themselves could not read; but when copies of the *Journal of Occurrences* were read to them, as sometimes happened, they expressed the most popeyed amazement. Why in bloody hell, they were wont to ask, would anybody go to all the trouble of raping a woman in Boston when there were so many there to be had for next to nothing? Nevertheless Samuel Adams wrote on.

It was an explosive situation; and soon it exploded.

CHAPTER THIRTEEN

Blood on the Snow

When troops arrived in Boston, their boots clacking, their voices raised in challenge, their gun butts thudding, the tremulous customsmen emerged blinking from Castle William like so many minute borers crawling out of the woodwork. Smuggling once again became a crime.

It was against these enforcement agents rather than the redcoats themselves that the people responded. The agents were hated. They could appear in public only because of the protective presence of the soldiers, and there was a great deal of snarling between them and the townspeople.

It is a fixed part of American mythology that the colonists of this time were virtually born and certainly brought up with muskets clutched in their chubby little fists, and that shooting was as natural to them as sneezing. That was not so. Most town-living colonists saw firearms only on a militia day, when the local boys would march and wheel on the square. Back by the frontier many a house might indeed have a gun mounted over its fireplace, as sentimental artists have assured us, but the frontier in 1770 was a long way from Boston. Firearms were *not* natural to the town-living colonists. They were thick, heavy, long things to be handled only with the greatest of care. Except in preparation for the final salute that marked the end of the exercise, for instance, the muskets the militia carried were never loaded. Nobody in his right mind would shoulder a loaded musket on parade. They were too dangerous, too uncertain. When it came to firing, reloading, firing again, the clumsiest Thomas Lobster could make a fool of any provincial. After all, the lobsterbacks had been trained for it, and their weapons were standard, with interchangeable parts.

About the redcoats' favorite weapon, the one they were famous for, the bayonet, Americans knew nothing. Properly handled, the bayonet was the best possible instrument for controlling crowds. Bostonians might scream at the sentries, for their leaders had assured them that a soldier could not fire his piece without first getting permission from a magistrate, but when that bright strip of steel was lowered, men were careful not to get too close.

Flare-ups occurred; and more than once, and especially at the Neck checkpoint, it was touch and go as to whether a rebellion would break out. Yet it was a customs informer rather than a redcoat who drew the first blood.

The nonimportation agreements were to expire January 1, 1770. The movement was already a dead letter in New York and Philadelphia, having, most merchants thought, outlived its usefulness. The Sons of Liberty in Boston resisted. The agreement, they said, had been *not to send to England* for any more material until January 1. However, the local merchants contended that the agreement had been only not to *sell* any English material until that time.

When the merchants tried to do business again, the Sons resorted to a crude blockade, posting a shop with a large hand that pointed to it, while over the hand was the word "IMPORTER." In addition, and if the merchant continued to stay open, they smashed the windows or else smeared them with mud or with excrement. They had large numbers of little boys to assist them in this important work. The boys thought it great fun.

Into such a scene in the North End, late in the morning of February 23, there strode the ominous figure of Ebenezer Richardson, a customs official who lived only about fifty yards away. The boys, with a few encouraging grown-ups, were pestering mild-mannered little Theophilus Lillie before his shop. When Richardson tried to tear down the "IMPORTER" sign, they turned on him with sticks and stones and snowballs, and chased him to his house.

Richardson had a vile temper, and he might have been drunk. Just in front of his doorway he was joined by a friend, a sailor out of work, George Wilmot, who swore that, by God, he'd stick with him if it meant killing somebody. The two took refuge in the house, where Richardson's wife and two small daughters trembled, and the boys outside began the pleasant task of smashing the windows. Richardson appeared in the open doorway and shook a musket at them, vowing that he would shoot. He didn't shoot; but then he showed up at a second-story window, again with a gun, which he aimed and snapped. At another window Wilmot did the same. The boys, all unabashed, went right on breaking windows.

Somebody started to ring the bell of the New Brick Church in Hanover Street nearby, and a few men drifted up, but it remained essentially a kids' show. They had broken open the front door, but they were afraid to go in. They hurled stones in instead.

Richardson appeared again, upstairs, crying that he would fire. Nobody believed him. He fired.

He had loaded the gun with swan shot, pellets about the size of peas, and he could hardly have missed at that distance, faced with such a crowd. A few of the bits of lead tore through a sailor's trousers, a few nicked a lad's knuckles, but most, between sixteen and twenty of them, went into the chest and abdomen of an eleven-year-old boy, Christopher Sneider.

They carried young Sneider to the home of a physician not far away, but there was nothing that could be done. He was dying.

Nobody had yet dared to go through Richardson's front door, but they battered down the back door. The attackers were all men now, the boys having been pushed aside, and they charged the embattled ones.

Wilmot surrendered readily, pointing out that the lock of the musket he held was broken, so that he could not have fired. Richardson held them off for a little while with a cutlass, but at last he was overwhelmed. The men were lucky they were not lynched. There was talk of it, and somebody, it was said, actually produced a rope. The reason cooler heads prevailed was because it was generally understood that, there being so many witnesses, the men would be hanged anyway. Richardson and Wilmot were thrown into jail.

The boy Christopher Sneider died at nine o'clock that night. His funeral, which started at the Liberty Tree and extended to the Granary Burying Ground, was held Monday, February 26. It was the most spectacular such ceremony ever seen in Boston. Samuel Adams, who stage-managed it, saw to that.

"Young as he was, he died in his Country's Cause," cried the Boston *Gazette*.

Now the radicals had a martyr.

One more thing that Bostonians had against their visitors was the fact that the officers, welcoming anything that would tend to keep the men busy, had given them permission to increase their niggardly earnings by working for civilians in off-hours. They worked, of course, for a low wage, glad to get even that, and the civilian laborers did not like it.

Patrick Walker, a private, was passing the huge rope works of John Gray the afternoon of Friday, March 2, when a man inside, one Sam Gray—no relation to the owner—called out to ask him if he wanted to do a little work. Walker quickly said that he did.

"Then you can clean out my shit-house," quoth Sam Gray.

Walker, furious, dared him to come out on the street and repeat that, and Gray said "sure," and came out.

Gray was popular at the rope walk. He was followed by fellow workers. Walker thought better of it, and beat a retreat. But Walker soon returned, coming from the barracks, and he was followed by some of *his* friends. This time the rope workers, before they went to the fray, picked up some woolder sticks.

A woolder stick was a necessity in the rope walks, or rope factories, that abounded in Boston. Made of hard wood, it was about 3½ to 4 feet long and about 2 inches thick in the middle, this thickness tapering, very gradually, to about 1 inch at each end. The ends were rounded. The woolder stick was used as a sort of lever to regulate the angle of lay when making thick rope, but it was ideal, too, for street fighting. It was something like an oversized nightstick.

Backed up by the woolder sticks, the rope workers prevailed. The 29th was not finished, however, and a large number of its men came back the next day, looking for trouble. Once again the men from Gray's triumphed. Only one soldier reported sick afterward, and he had a concussion, but soldiers only did report the most serious wounds from street fighting, for fear of punishment.

The next day was the Lord's Day, so nobody fought. It was understood throughout Boston, though, that the battle had only begun.

It snowed that night, heavily. In the morning the town was found to have been plastered with paper warnings supposedly signed by soldiers. They soon disappeared. There was always something strange about them, and one theory is that they were put up by the Sons of Liberty with the deliberate purpose of promoting a general fight for which the soldiers could later be blamed.

Each side was as edgy as a racehorse, and quivered with suspicion.

Monday, perhaps because of the snow, which was almost a foot deep, was quiet. The disturbance did not start until night.

There were no street lamps in Boston. It was a clear and cold night, with the moon in its first quarter. Besides the snow there was a great deal of broken ice.

The British Army had recently lowered its minimum height requirement for recruits from 5 feet 10 inches to 5 feet 8 inches, then to 5 feet 6 inches, and more lately to 5 feet 4 inches. Private Hugh White, the sentry posted in front of the customs house at King Street and the Royal Exchange Lane that night, was probably not even 5 feet 4 inches. It is on record that he was a very short man. He also had a short man's truculence. When boys began to throw snowballs at him, daring him to shoot off his gun, and when men, idlers, backed up these youngsters, White feared that he might be carried off bodily and perhaps dumped into the bay. Drastic action was needed, he thought. He singled out a particularly sassy lad and slapped the side of his face with his gun butt. The boy ran, bleeding, crying in pain, but the rest of the crowd only edged closer. More snowballs flew, some with rocks in them.

White called for help.

The bell at the Brattle Street Church began to ring, and that of the New Brick Church. In the daytime the church bells of Boston might be rung for a wedding, a funeral, almost anything, but when they sounded *at night*, it ordinarily meant but one thing—fire.

There was no fire department. There were no regulars, only volunteers. Pieces of apparatus, such as hose spools, pumping engines, and bucket carriers, were scattered here and there in public or semipublic places, and now men hastened to drag them into the streets, adding to the confusion.

Despite the Mutiny Act, the British Army was paying for its quarters in Boston. The Common was too cold now, and Castle William, though large enough, and technically a part of the town, was too far away to be of any service in the event of street riots. As it was, the 14th was garrisoned, in full, in Murray's sugar warehouse near Dock Square. The 29th had small scattered sleeping spots—in Water Lane, Atkinson Street, and elsewhere. The main guard was right in the center of town, facing, in fact, the Town House—that is, City Hall —in front of which had been placed two fat brass cannons. When members of the General Court came out of their meetings, the first things they would see were those guns, pointed at them. This, Samuel Adams had contended angrily, could be construed as a threat; but the guns remained.

The 29th was on duty that night, and the officer of the guard was Captain Thomas Preston. He was forty years old, an Irishman, and by everybody's account a solid citizen, not one to get excited. He was having a drink at the British Coffee House when word was brought to him of the trouble in front of the customs house. He went immediately to the main guard, just around the corner from that building.

There he paused, trying to learn what it was all about. It *could* be, after all, a fire. But the noise that reached him was not the roar and spitting of flames. Was this a real uprising, a planned affair? If he went out into the crowd, his presence there might make matters worse, for he was, of course, in uniform. On the other hand, if he didn't go, he might lose his sentry, poor little Hugh White.

He summoned a corporal's guard. The corporal was William Wemms, the privates Carroll, Warren, Kilroy, Montgomery, Hartigan, and McCauley. All excepting the corporal were grenadiers—that is, tall men made to seem the taller by their high steeple hats. The muskets they carried were not loaded, but they had fixed their bayonets.

Captain Preston went with them.

Here was chaos. Those in the back pushed forward, yammering, while those close in did all that they could to keep away—but never far away—from the leveled bayonets. The redcoats formed in a semicircle to protect the little one-man sentry box, up until this time White's only place of refuge. Captain Preston stood between them and the crowd, jostled this way and that, pleading with the men to go home.

In nearby Dock Square a tall man in a red cloak and wearing a large white wig harangued the crowd and urged immediate action. Nobody ever did identify this man, though many heard him.

Acting Governor Hutchinson was called from his handsome, rebuilt house, and he hurried through the noise-shaken streets to the Town House. This took courage.

The men sheltering the sentry box loaded their guns. It was done with an alacrity and snap that never failed to astound Americans, who still had to measure powder and cut and weigh lead before they could ram home a charge.

Men came from all directions, yelling and cursing. Some carried clubs, others rocks or large chunks of ice. There were no muskets or pistols as far as anybody could see, and no swords. Some of the boys were armed with nothing more warlike than cat sticks, which were halves of broom handles, later to be called catty sticks, the same thing that city boys use today when they play stickball.

There might have been two hundred men and boys there in the tiny square in front of the customs house. There might have been more. There were as many as there could be.

Captain Preston's first thought was for the safety of his sentry. Now he paused. If he gave an order to march back to the main guard, it might be taken for a sign of fear and might result in a rush. Also, it would leave the customs house unprotected. There was a great deal of money in that building —the King's money.

A brickbat, or perhaps it was a hurled cudgel—we will never know—hit Hugh Montgomery in the shoulder and knocked him down. He dropped his musket as he fell. In an instant he was up again, and had snatched it up too. Swearing furiously, he aimed the piece at the crowd and pulled the trigger.

Then they were all shooting, not in a volley, as they had been trained to do—"controlled fire power" was the military vogue at the moment—but here and there erratically. It sounded like doors being slammed in a large empty house.

One man in the crowd dropped, then another, and another. Five crumpled forms showed blackly against the snow when the crowd, appalled, fell back. One spectator said that even then he could not believe that there had been real shooting; he supposed in his excitement that the soldiers had put no balls into their guns, only powder and wadding, and he thought at first that those black blurs on the ground were not men at all but only greatcoats left by men who had fled.

They were in fact Patrick Carr, recently arrived from Ireland, an apprentice to a maker of leather aprons; James Caldwell, a ship's mate; Sam Gray, the same ropemaker who had commanded Patrick Walker to clean out his privy; Samuel Maverick, apprentice to an ivory turner and only seventeen years old; and Crispus Attucks, a huge, six-foot-two mulatto, perhaps part Indian. Carr and Maverick were still alive, but barely. And there were another six men wounded. An ounce-and-a-quarter chunk of lead, fired at close quarters, can cause a terrible wound. There was a great deal of blood.

The soldiers had reloaded, once again not at command, as they had been taught, but each man for himself. When they saw the sullen black mass of townsmen returning, slowly, shufflingly, but with the certainty of a tide, they leveled their muskets again. Preston, in front of them now, knocked up the muzzles.

The townspeople were not looking for any further trouble. They only wanted to carry away their dead and wounded.

Preston marched his men back to the main guard. He set up a squad in position for street fighting, each file to consist of one kneeling, one stooping, one upright, and sent a sergeant with several privates to seek out the colonel.

For almost an hour it looked as though hell might erupt again at any moment, and so thick were the crowds that this time it would certainly have resulted in large-scale slaughter. But after a while the men went home, leaving red blotches in the snow.

CHAPTER FOURTEEN

Uneasy Lie the Prisoners

Thomas Hutchinson got no sleep that night. He had taken his life in his hands when he eeled his way through teeming narrow streets to the Town House, where from a balcony he addressed the crowd. Later, indoors, he conferred with Lieutenant Colonel Maurice Carr of the 29th and "Steel Breeches" Dalrymple of the 14th, who ranked Carr. After that it was dawn, and he called a meeting of his Council.

Meanwhile Samuel Adams was calling a town meeting.

The Boston town meeting had become, quite simply, a revolutionary committee. It was not even called town meeting any longer; it was just The Body. Hutchinson had forbidden it, but no attention was paid to him. The Body was flexible. It would meet anywhere, at the drop of a tricorn. It met now, early in the morning of Tuesday, March 6, at Faneuil Hall and appointed a committee to demand that all the British troops be withdrawn from the town and stationed in Castle William. The chairman: Samuel Adams.

The committee did not need horses. The Town House was virtually across the street. Adams led the way, his lips twitching, his head ashake.

The councillors wore scarlet robes and big white wigs. In the middle of them, doing his best to assume a Rhadamanthine calm, sat Thomas Hutchinson, Lieutenant Colonel Dalrymple at his side.

Adams made his demand. Hutchinson consulted for some time, in whispers, with Dalrymple and with certain of the councillors. Then he proposed that the offending regiment only, the 29th, should be shifted to Castle William, while the 14th remained in town.

Samuel Adams shook his head. "Both regiments or none," he said. But he did consent to place the proposition before The Body.

Back across the snow they marched, this time to the Old South Church, for Faneuil Hall was not large enough to hold everybody. It was only a matter of minutes for the meeting to reinstruct the chairman of the committee and to endorse his stand overwhelmingly.

Back through the snow they went, Adams' hands fluttering like bone-colored birds. "Both regiments or none!"

Hutchinson and Dalrymple and the others consulted uneasily. Hutchinson just at first had asserted that he did not have the power to transfer the troops. This excuse Samuel Adams brushed aside. He pointed out that according to the Massachusetts Bay charter, which he quoted, the governor of the province was also commander in chief of all the King's forces stationed there.

And now at last the acting governor acted. He bowed his head. Both regiments, he promised, would be moved.

It was a stunning victory for the Patriots.

Thereafter, in England, the 14th and the 29th were to be called the Sam Adams regiments.

Captain Preston surrendered, along with his soldiers, later that morning. They were thrust into the dark Boston town jail, which they shared with two others who faced the charge of murder—Ebenezer Richardson and George Wilmot.

The shooting had not cleared the air. Each side—the angry townspeople, confronted by the equally angry customs officials and the military men—was firm in its belief that the other side had concocted a dastardly plot.

The military advanced many reasons for delaying the movement to Castle William. Dalrymple wrote a long report of the affair to General Gage, who was back in New York, and asked for orders. He *implied* that he really should wait for those orders before he led his men to Castle William, but it took seventeen days to get an answer from New York and the colonel was not permitted that much time. He seems really to have been afraid, as his men certainly were, that there would be a united uprising of the populace.

Dalrymple doggedly refused to call the events of the night of March 5 a massacre. Rather, he referred to them as "the Scuffle." Nevertheless, after he had stalled for almost two weeks, but before orders had come from New York, he did withdraw his men. Most of the customs agents went with them—though one, a man named Jesse Savil, was set upon in the street in nearby Gloucester by a gang of men who had blackened their faces. Savil was stripped and hot-tarred and marched around town that way.

The streets of Boston, however, were quieter and seemingly safer than they had been when the soldiers were there.

Depositions were taken on both sides. The military authorities, with little else to do, got theirs wrapped up first and sent them to England, while a committee headed by Samuel Adams was still compiling statements calculated to prove the other side of the case. The Patriots' version probably would not have been credited anyway. It certainly *shouldn't* have been. It was a potpourri of lies and hysterical stories that bore almost no resemblance to the truth. Adams outdid even his *Journal of Occurrences* in imagination, and he had no trouble finding what he wanted, for townsmen by the score came in with horrendous tales. They persisted in their belief that there had been a plot to kill large numbers of honest Bostonians, and they bolstered this story with affidavits taken from townsmen who testified that they had heard soldiers or customs agents utter dire threats. For a long while the committeemen relied upon various statements to the effect that somebody had been seen firing out of the windows of the customs house while the shooting took place in the street. This was almost universally believed, though the principal witnesses in its favor were a half-witted apprentice and a fourteen-year-old French boy, a servant, who kept changing his story.

Henry Pelham, the talented half-brother of the young artist John Copley, drew a cartoon of the "massacre." It shows seven soldiers (there were eight, actually) firing a volley (there was nothing like a volley) at the command of an officer waving a sword. The soldiers all wear three-cornered hats, though in fact six were grenadiers, who were issued steeple hats only. In the background, over a shop, is a sign that reads "Butchers Hall," though there was no such sign in that part of King Street. Pelham, it would seem, merely wished to remind the viewer that *butchery* was going on. Moreover, in one window of the customs house there is a puff of smoke.

Paul Revere, the rider, the silversmith, a staunch Patriot, somehow got hold of this cartoon, and he engraved it, printed it, and sold it, making a lot of money. Pelham, who had not been consulted, objected vehemently. The matter was settled out of court, but the cartoon, a bald-faced piece of propaganda (the original is in the Boston Public Library today), must have affected the thinking of thousands.

The hoopla attending young Sneider's funeral paled before the show that Adams and his associates provided when they had *four* martyrs to bury. Upward of two thousand mourners were reported to have followed the train to the Granary Burial Grounds, though rumor had it that some of them were repeaters, who got into line two or even three times. Adams had already arranged, through his instrument the town meeting, to have the day of the shooting, March 5, declared a municipal holiday. It was his plan to stage a full-time lest-we-forget rally that day each year, together with an oration, music, and of course a sermon.

Three of the "Scuffle" victims had died immediately. Young Maverick, who had been running away from the scene at the time he was hit, expired that same night. Patrick Carr, however, lingered for more than a week, dying at last on March 15.

Carr disappointed the Patriots by insisting that the redcoats were justified in shooting as they did and when they did, their lives being endangered. The best that Adams could do about that, with the approval of the full committee, was to point out that, after all, Carr had been brought up a Roman Catholic, so what else could you expect?

Delay was not then a built-in part of American justice. It still was something new, and as such it was resented. Thomas Hutchinson remained nominally the chief justice of the Massachusetts superior court, but because he was acting as governor he did not serve in that capacity in this case. The justices who would try Captain Preston and the soldiers—and presumably Richardson and Wilmot—were four in number, Peter Oliver, John Cushing, Edmund Trowbridge, and Benjamin Lynde, the last being the acting chief justice. Only one of these men, Trowbridge, was a lawyer, but all were Loyalists who viewed with a jaundiced eye the usurping behavior of the town meeting, The Body. Their statutory term began on March 13, but since two of them, Trowbridge and Cushing, were ill, the court did not sit then.

Meanwhile, Samuel Adams, assisted by many of the clergymen in town, was raising a most un-Christian clamor for blood. He demanded of the acting governor that he appoint two temporary judges, so that the soldiers' case could be tried while passions were still hot. This Hutchinson refused to do.

The case was further complicated by the fact that the grand jury had seen fit to indict, besides the soldiers, four civilians, all of them connected with the customs service, and all accused of plotting against the lives of the various martyrs. The case against them was pitifully weak, and they were released in £400 bail apiece.

There was dark talk of "Porteousing" the prisoners if the judges didn't sentence them to death. Captain John Porteous had been the commander of the guard at an execution in Edinburgh in 1736, and when the crowd became unruly, or his men thought it did, they had fired into it, killing several persons. Porteous had been tried for this, convicted, and sentenced to hang, but had been reprieved. Free, he had been set upon by a mob that lynched him.

Six extra guards were stationed around the Boston jail now, night and day. There was talk of transferring some or all of the prisoners to Castle William or perhaps to one of the warships.

The prosecuting official was to have been Attorney General Jonathan Sewell, a staunch Loyalist, but he suddenly learned that he had important business out of town. He left Boston. The court appointed the solicitor general, Samuel Quincy, as special prosecutor. He, too, was a Loyalist.

Richardson and Wilmot had not been able to persuade any lawyer to represent them, so it was necessary for the court to appoint one. This the court did, but the appointee, a man named Fitch, managed to squirm out of it, though he might have been trapped if John Adams and his young associate, Josiah Quincy, had not just at this time come forward to offer their services for the defense—the defense, that is, not only of Richardson and Wilmot but also of Preston and the soldiers.

This seems strange at first. John Adams in matters political was of his cousin's way of thinking, and Samuel Adams was splenetically clamoring for the death penalty. However, John Adams liked to picture himself as a man sacrificing his career by thus embracing an unpopular cause. In truth, he was incurably romantic, a dreamer; fighting single-handed against great odds fascinated him. He envisioned himself as a crusader. In later years he was to set it down that members of the King's party had talked him into heading the defense, contrary to his own inclinations, but we know now that it was the Patriots, his own cousin most of all.

Why was this? Why should the Man of the Town Meeting urge his own relative to defend men he himself fervently believed to be guilty? It could only be that he was so sure of a conviction that he sought to make himself and the party he worked for seem the more noble by drafting the best lawyer in town to take the other side. That is the only possible explanation. The cases against Richardson and the soldiers seemed to the Patriots watertight. They had no doubt that these men would hang, no matter who defended them.

Richardson in fact was convicted, though only after the crowd in the packed courtroom had jeered Justice Oliver when he summed up and had shouted ugly warnings to the jury as it retired. Wilmot was acquitted. There is no doubt that the four justices believed that Richardson should have been acquitted too, but they could see no way to upset the jury's verdict, and so they simply refused for the present to pass sentence. They would have no choice about that sentence. The law demanded the death penalty. But they postponed it until May 29, hoping against hope, it must be supposed, that a miracle would occur to release them from the hateful duty. Then, not having even considered the case against the soldiers, they adjourned to Charlestown, where they started to sit on April 7. They sat too, as required by law, in various places in Maine and then in a part of Massachusetts, and all that took a long time. During most of May they were sitting in Plymouth and Barnstable and other towns in the district. When they returned to Boston on May 29 to sentence Richardson, there were only two of them, for Trowbridge was ill and Oliver had been thrown from his horse. Court was adjourned until the thirty-first.

Meanwhile, John Fleeming, who had been John Mein's partner, was warned that the Sons of Liberty had marked him for chastisement, and he fled to Castle William. On the night of May 18 three customs agents were taken out of their houses by men who did not trouble to blacken their faces. One agent was tarred and feathered and paraded in his underclothes for four hours, though it was a cold night. The other two, after having been scared half to death, were released.

The superior court sat again on May 31, and two of its members still being absent, it adjourned to its statutory date of August 28. That would surely give the popular rage a chance to cool.

The prosecution and the defense, between them, decided to try Captain Preston separately from the eight soldiers. This might seem to make the problem of the defense more difficult, if not insoluble, for if Preston was found guilty of crying "Fire!" then the men were innocent, having only obeyed orders, whereas if Preston was acquitted, if a jury decided that he had *not* given the command to shoot, then the men were guilty. John Adams did not seem to worry about this.

By the time Preston was brought to trial it was October. Boston was a port town, and undoubtedly some of the witnesses, mariners, were no longer available. It was not this, though, that brought about Preston's acquittal. It was John Adams' brilliant defense and, even more, the weak prosecution. The prosecution, for instance, while it did not use up all of its challenges, permitted the drawing of a jury that did not contain a single Son of Liberty but did contain five acknowledged Loyalists.

The trial lasted five days.

When the soldiers' petition to be tried with Captain Preston was turned down, they lost confidence in the court. They needn't have. Adams and Quincy were just as effective, the prosecutor just as wobbly. The defense lawyers pointed out that although there had been eight soldiers with eight muskets, only seven shots were fired. Montgomery and Kilroy were the only ones definitely known to have discharged their guns, and they were convicted of manslaughter. The other six, since it was not known which of them had fired the other five shots, and since an accused man should be given the benefit of the doubt, were acquitted. Moreover, Kilroy and Montgomery, though quite possibly unable to spell cat, were permitted to "plead their clergy" by reciting the carefully memorized so-called Neck Verse, the first verse of the 51st Psalm—"Have mercy upon me, O God, according to thy loving-kindness: according unto the multitude of thy tender mercies blot out my transgressions"—and were thus excluded from the death sentence. Instead they were branded on the left thumb.

As for Ebenezer Richardson, once again the government protected its own. He was quietly pardoned in England, the great delay having allowed the time for this, and then *very* quietly transferred to Philadelphia.

CHAPTER FIFTEEN

Strange Yokefellows

Man, Aristotle has told us, is a political animal. But we know that politics makes strange yokefellows. Politics is not a predictable business.

It would seem that when he confronted the governor and Council, Samuel Adams was at the peak of his career. He had faced up to the British Empire, and the Empire had backed away.

In fact, an undercurrent had already formed, a movement of which the hissing of the combers gave no hint. Adams, far from being all-powerful, was losing his political grip.

The very day of the Massacre, March 5, 1770, Parliament in London started to consider the repeal of the Townshend duties, which had proved incapable of raising any appreciable amount of money but had cost English merchants, through the American nonimportation movement, millions. Parliament did indeed repeal them, all except the one on tea. In accordance with the Declaratory Act of 1766, Parliament still kept the right to tax the colonies, but for the present Americans could only see that most of the taxes had been removed under pressure, and they deduced from this that a time for peace and quiet had come. Something like an era of economic good feeling set in. Samuel Adams' impassioned protests seemed old-fashioned and far away, not to be taken seriously. The

Tories in America, in Massachusetts itself, even in Boston, took a new lease on life.

Nothing more was heard about the possibility of sending Samuel Adams and perhaps one or two others to England for trial. Nobody seemed any longer to care.

For almost a year and a half the American colonies were not even mentioned in the House of Commons.

Castle William being overcrowded, and there seeming little likelihood that Boston would consent to take the soldiers back, General Gage moved the hated 29th to New Jersey. As for the 14th, Bostonians seldom saw any of its members anymore.

The acting governor, Thomas Hutchinson, obeying an order he received from Lord Hillsborough, caused the General Court of Massachusetts to move its meeting place from Boston, where it had always been, to Cambridge, where there wasn't room for it. The purpose of this move was to weaken the authority of the Boston Seat. Members of that delegation opposed it bitterly, though they could not deny the right of the governor to order it. This move to the Philosophy Room at Harvard was inconvenient for all concerned, including the college faculty, which also protested.

Ever since Francis Bernard was created a baronet, there had been rumors that the acting governor, Hutchinson, would soon be appointed governor. That is what happened. Hutchinson's brother-in-law, Andrew Oliver, secretary of the province, now became the lieutenant governor, thus keeping the post in the family, while Thomas Flucker, a dedicated King's Man, became secretary.

This change shook Samuel Adams. Bernard had been a bluff English squire, easily understood and as easily circumvented. Hutchinson, in Adams' eyes, was a renegade. Adams could not subscribe to the easy belief that in appointing to the governorship a Massachusetts man the ministers were making a bid for conciliation. Things would *not* be better under such a man, he stormed. He feared Hutchinson, though he affected to despise him.

You compare him to Julius Caesar, that publick Executioner of his Countrys Rights [he wrote March 25, 1771, to James Warren]. He has, it is true, Caesars Ambition and Lust of Power; but who ever yet suspected that he had Caesars courage? Recollect the time when he was oblig'd to abandon his Troops, by which he had hoped to awe the People: It was then, if Fancy deceived me not, I observ'd his Knees to tremble. I thought I saw his face grow pale (and I enjoyd the Sight) at the Appearance of the determined Citizens peremptorily demanding the Redress of Grievances.

In his official correspondence with Governor Hutchinson Adams no longer called it the Town House. It was the State House now, which made the new governor squirm. Adams would refer to the laws of the land, rather than to the provincial laws; he would write of the debates in the assembly as "Parliamentary" debates, and he always called the charter the "compact."

This annoyed Hutchinson, as he confessed to friends, the more so because there wasn't anything he could do about it; but it did not further the Patriot cause. The fact was that in Thomas Hutchinson Samuel Adams had met something like his match. Bernard, cornered, would huffily have taken refuge in his dignity as the representative of the King, but Hutchinson would stand right up to Adams, answering him in his own language.

As "Candidus" in the *Gazette* Adams still carried on, and indeed he even raised his voice:

If therefore we are voluntarily silent while this single duty on tea is continued, or do any act, however innocent, simply considered, which may be construed by the tools of administration (some of whom appear to be fruitful in invention) as an acquiescence in the measure, we are in extreme hazard; if ever we are so distracted as to consent to it, we are undone. . . . The most zealous advocates for the measures of administration, will not pretend to say, that these troops and these ships are sent here to protect America, or to carry into execution any one plan, form'd for the honor or advantage of Great-Britain. It would be some alleviation, if we could be convinced that they were sent here with any other design than to insult us.

The nonimportation movement sagged. The other colonies, even Virginia, seemed to have become satisfied with the place in which they found themselves, and to deplore the pauseless pushing ahead of the New England "Saints."

Even at home, among his own people, Samuel Adams felt his influence slip. The Massachusetts colonial agent in London, Dennys DeBernt, had died, and there was a movement to replace him with Benjamin Franklin, who, though a resident of Pennsylvania, had been born in Boston, and who was on the scene. Samuel Adams, who disliked and distrusted Franklin, opposed this movement, favoring rather Arthur Lee of Virginia, a younger brother of Richard Henry Lee; but he was defeated two to one.

His companions in the great struggle, it seemed to him, were losing force. James Otis had gone entirely mad. James Bowdoin, Thomas Cushing, and Joseph Hawley appeared to waver. Worst of all, just at this time Samuel Adams was to lose his protégé, John Hancock.

As the lines became more clearly drawn, as open warfare loomed, both sides began to wheedle the rich. Property carried with it an immense prestige. The more a man owned, was the theory, the bigger was his interest in the welfare of the state. In general the Tories made up the rich man's party, and the Whigs were poor. There were many exceptions. The wealthiest man in the colonies was Charles Carroll of Carrollton, Maryland, who was to espouse the cause of independence. Two extremely active generals in the Continental Army-to-come, Philip Schuyler and George Washington, were very rich men.

New Englanders were often accused by residents of the middle and southern colonies of being "levelers," that is, of believing that all men are not necessarily born into certain fixed classes. The New Englanders indignantly denied this.

John Hancock was undoubtedly the richest man in New England.

Here was a peacock. He strutted and swished, iridescent, admiring himself. He owned a great deal of Boston—half the town, it was popularly said—and a wharf and many vessels. He had inherited all this from an uncle, Thomas Hancock.

The nephew was unmarried and ambitious. He liked show. When he fared forth, it was in a carriage, and with outriders. The neighbors called him King John.

Such a man, it could be assumed, would gravitate to the King's party, a pretentious group with its airs and its privileges, its snuffboxes, its lace. Thomas Hutchinson had gone out of his way to woo John Hancock, and once he had become governor of Massachusetts, he offered Hancock the colonelcy of the Boston Cadets, a crack company of well-connected boys and young men who used to drill on the Common to the ohs and ahs of their elders. Hancock was delighted with this honor, for he fancied himself as a military leader, though he did not have a day of training. He bought them all new uniforms.

The Hancock fortune, however, had been founded on smuggling, and John could be counted upon to have some respect for the methods so successfully employed by his late uncle. Moreover, when he had first begun to thrust a tentative head into politics, it was Samuel Adams rather than Thomas Hutchinson who glittered with the sheen of success, while the Tories seemed a tired-out lot. Adams jumped at the chance to annex this personage to his party, and soon the two were inseparable.

Hancock for his part was proud of his distinguished friend and associate, who in fact taught him a great deal, more than he would have been able to learn anywhere else, about politics. He liked him so much that he had young Copley paint both their portraits.

The sight of this ill-matched pair, the one so sloppy, the other dapper, amused Boston. The irreverent John Mein was wont to refer to Hancock as Johnny Dupe, or the Milch-Cow, and to picture him as a creature with long ears, suggestive of the jackass, while it was said that Samuel Adams "led him about like an ape."

Word of this might have reached Hancock. Or it could be that with the unexpected return of prosperity, the coming of the so-called Era of Good Feeling, he had begun to believe that he should give more time to his business. At any rate, and whatever the reason, he waxed noticeably less radical, and there was a coolness between him and his one-time mentor.

No matter. Samuel Adams never changed *his* course, never modified *his* opinions, or wearied of the fight.

CHAPTER SIXTEEN

Tea

What was it that halted Samuel Adams in his political descent? What blocked him at the last minute, on the very lip of the trash barrel? Tea. Yes, it was tea that did it.

The first English-speaking immigrants to America had not had the tea habit. They had never even heard of tea, for England was behind most of the rest of the Western world in this respect. Only the Dutch, founding Nieuw Amsterdam, brought tea with them, for they were intrepid travelers and willing to try anything new.

The beginnings of tea are fuzzy, misted by antiquity, but we do know that it was grown and drunk for many centuries in China, and then in Japan, and in Java and Malaya, before anybody from Europe noticed it. It was taken rather as a medicine than as a stimulant, so that the taste was muffled by herbs and spices—cloves, cardamom, fennel, cinnamon, nutmeg, aniseed. Indeed, when it was at last adopted by the English they sold it in apothecary shops.

Philip II of Spain carried on his arms the legend *Non Sufficit Orbis*, "The World is Not Enough," as well he might and so it seemed, for he owned more of this habitable globe than ever had Alexander of Macedon. His father, the Emperor Charles V, when he retired to a monastery had left Philip a good part of Europe as well as most of the recently discovered new world of America. When Philip died, in 1598, leaving all of this to *his* son, another Philip, a weakling, the men who ruled England under Elizabeth whooshed in relief. There would be no more Armadas. In that same year the Dutch and the Portuguese, who controlled the trade to the Far East, got together and decided to raise the wholesale price of that trade's chief item, pepper, from three to eight shillings a pound. This was too much for the English, who now took steps to get a little of the fabled riches of the Orient for themselves rather than at second hand. A group of merchants in London organized the East India Company, which received its charter on the last day of 1600.

Tea (*Camellia sinensis*) is an evergreen shrub that grows to be thirty feet tall if you let it, though it is customarily kept down to three or four. It was a novelty at first, handled in very small quantities. Of the three nonalcoholic drinks that were suddenly offered to the Western world, the first was cocoa, introduced by the Spaniards from America, along with tobacco; the second, from China, was tea, while a very close third was "the little brown berry of Arabia," coffee. Tea did not catch on as quickly as the others, and for a long time Europeans went on thinking of it as a medicine. Also, it was expensive.

Not until 1720, a whole century after the landing near Plymouth Rock, was tea sent to North America; yet by the 1760's some 1 million pounds a year were being sent.

It came in chests of about 450 pounds gross, usually lead-lined, weighing some 360 pounds net. There were also half-chests and quarter-chests, but they were used only with Hyson, Singlo, and Souchong tea, for which there was little call in America. By far the greatest part of the tea to America, and all of what the smugglers handled, was black stuff from the Bohea Hills of China.

Some of this tea came directly from Holland, and some came by way of St. Eustatius ("Staysha"), sometimes called the Golden Rock, a Dutch open port in the West Indies. Tea was a product conveniently smuggled. Easily concealed, virtually indestructible, it would fit in here and there, a little in this place, a little in that. It *filled out* cargos, as a rule. It was not often a cargo in itself.

Indeed, much of this tea was smuggled into the colonies *twice*. Tea drinking came to be general, all the way from Georgia to Maine, and when a shortage was threatened at any point along the coast, the watchful dealers in Boston, New York, Philadelphia, Annapolis, upon receipt of a large consignment of tea, would reship a part of it by small coastwise vessels to the place where it was needed. Double-smuggling was a business that called for alert dealers with fast vessels, but the profits were high. Thomas Wharton of Philadelphia and John Waddell of New York, sometimes as partners, were especially active in this trade.

There were to be other East India companies after the one that Elizabeth chartered—Dutch, French, Danish, Austrian, Swedish, Spanish, Prussian—but the English one was always the master. Its charter was amended from time to time, and it was granted extraordinary privileges. Its first vessels were not large for such a long voyage, most of them being of 499 tons burthen. The reason for this was that the law of that time, Elizabeth's time, stipulated that any vessel of 500 tons or more must carry a chaplain, and the East India Company directors, while always willing to spend vast sums of money on relatives or friends—or upon themselves—did not see why they should help to support the cloth. Anyway, they soon arranged to have that law repealed, after which they used enormous vessels.

The American trade was something that the East India Company did not touch, at first. It was handled through small English and American merchants and Dutch smugglers. In England itself, however, the Honourable East India Company enjoyed a monopoly. This of course led to smuggling there too. In the 1760's it was said that about one third of the tea drunk in England had never had duty paid on it.

The company was not doing well, for it was squeezed by greed. In 1772 it already owed the British government £1 million, though it had just passed a 12½ percent stock dividend, and the following year it borrowed £1.4 million more from the government, again paying 12½ percent to its shareholders. The interest on the £2.4 million was at 4 percent. Such were the anfractuosities of eighteenth-century English finance.

Powerful though it was, and adept at the turning out of nabobs, an empire in itself, the East India Company faced bankruptcy. With its thousands of shareholders, this would have amounted to a national catastrophe. The company simply must not be permitted to fall. Such a crash assuredly would carry the cabinet with it.

The twenty-four directors, after a great deal of soul-searching, came up with a suggestion: The company should be given a monopoly on the tea trade to America.

In warehouses in London alone it had stored some 17 million tons of tea, on which a drawback of 7½ pence a pound already had been paid or was due. The directors ingenuously proposed that the government waive the drawback and grant the company permission to ship this tea, from time to time, to America, where a threepence-a-pound import would be levied by the government. Englishmen and Scots were already paying sixpence a pound tax on the tea they drank. Americans would therefore get it, the same tea, cheaper—as cheap as the Dutch could supply it illegally.

The plan seemed foolproof. Bankruptcy would be averted. Smuggling would be stopped, or virtually stopped. The government would get a tax where there was no tax now. The Americans would have the cheapest tea possible, just about. And *better* tea.

The company would transport the tea itself, and it would appoint and control the American agents who retailed it.

Parliament when it repealed the other Townshend duties —on paint, glass, red lead, white lead—had refrained *by one vote* from including tea, largely because of the conviction of so many members that some manner of colonial tax had to be kept up if only to remind the colonists that the mother country had a right to tax them.

It was thought at the beginning of the session [of 1773] that the American duty on tea would be taken off [Benjamin Franklin wrote to Thomas Cushing]. But now the wise scheme is to take off so much duty here as will make tea cheaper in America than foreigners can supply us, and confine the duty there, to keep up the exercise of the right. . . . They have no idea that any people can act from any other principle but that of interest; and they believe that three pence in a pound of tea, of which one does perhaps drink ten pounds in a year, is sufficient to overcome all the patriotism of an American.

Franklin saw it right. It had never occurred to the East India Company directors and the statesmen at Whitehall that anybody might object to being put under a monopoly, a monopoly moreover that had a record of corruption and violence, of double-dealing and avarice, or that anybody would resent an illegal tax.

The protest that rose from the other side of the sea fairly astounded these conniving men.

Seventeen seventy-two was Samuel Adams' low point. In the elections for the Boston Seat on May 6 of that year there were 723 voters who each cast four ballots, of which Thomas Cushing got 699, John Hancock 690, William Phillips 688, and Samuel Adams only 505. He was in again; but he had run at the bottom of his ticket.

No matter. The tea men and the tax men would save him.

CHAPTER SEVENTEEN

A Man with a Twinkle in His Eye

It was not possible that Samuel Adams should trust a man with a twinkle in his eye. He and Benjamin Franklin were devoted to the Patriot cause, and they were fine writers who used their talents for the benefit of liberty, justice, and when the moment came, independence. They were to work together in the Continental Congress, but at the time that Parliament, without any division, almost without a look, passed the Tea Act of May 10, 1773, these two had never met.

Adams did not seek a meeting. He had heard enough, he thought, about Franklin. Could he confide in and confer with a man who loved wine and lively women, rich food, late hours, a man who had solemnly proposed in a Philadelphia newspaper that the American colonies send rattlesnakes to the mother country in return for the convicted criminals the mother country persisted in sending to *them*, one snake for one scoundrel, indefinitely? Could Vindex, Publicus, etc., take seriously a writer who had written so feelingly on farts and farting; who had advised a young correspondent that if he really wished to take a mistress it would be best to take one who was well along in years, and for eight reasons, the eighth being "They are so grateful!" and who had not only failed to hide his illegitimate son, William, but had aided the lad to get the governorship of New Jersey? No, it was not to be.

119

Samuel Adams, though he scorned to preen himself on paper, took his task seriously enough. He could never have dreamed of the hoaxes that Dr. Franklin delighted in, like, for instance, the Edict of the King of Prussia, which appeared all unexpectedly one fine day in the London press.

The Edict was elaborate, and it was pompous, as might have been expected from a Prussian monarch. The island of Great Britain, it pointed out, had originally been settled by Germans (Angles, Saxons, Jutes, Frisians), and since nothing had ever been done to separate the two countries he, the King of Prussia, assumed that the inhabitants of that land, the descendants of the original settlers, remained his subjects. He would, therefore, impose upon them the following taxes and restrictions—and there followed a thinly disguised list of the American complaints against British rule, including the prohibition of intercolonial commerce, the ban on ironworks, forbiddance of the manufacture of felt hats, and many others.

Even after they had passed this part of the Edict, many readers still did not see the point but supposed that they were in truth reading an announcement of their own enslavement. There were some, early Colonel Blimps, who purpled and pounded the table and cried that by God the beggar couldn't talk to *us* that way.

The Edict of the King of Prussia caused much merriment, but if those effete snobs, the English friends of Dr. Franklin, really did think it funny, Samuel Adams (for the thing was republished in some American papers) was not amused.

Franklin had made a good agent for Pennsylvania. He was a hard worker, and he was respected and even loved in the highest circles. The soul of geniality, he did not easily draw his dagger against a political foe, but the Earl of Hillsborough was an exception.

Hillsborough was the first Secretary of State for the Colonies, and the man who had given the American cause such a boost when he sought to quash the Massachusetts Circular

Letter. He too did not like or trust the beaming, white-haired Dr. Franklin, and when Franklin was appointed by the Massachusetts General Court to succeed Dennys DeBernt as agent for that province, Hillsborough refused to recognize this appointment or to receive Franklin. Franklin did not argue. Instead, he went quietly to work among his friends, and very soon, despite his family connections, the Right Honourable The Earl of Hillsborough found himself out of a job. Nobody liked him anyway. He had lasted four years, which was too long. Undoubtedly if Franklin had not acted as he did when he did, the earl would have been ousted anyway, for the King detested him.

Franklin had suggested William Legge, Earl of Dartmouth, as Hillsborough's successor, and Dartmouth was duly chosen. He was an intensely religious man, a Methodist (Dartmouth College, originally an Indian school, was to be named in his honor). He was cautious, conservative, and he might have been shocked by the behavior of the Americans, but he had faith in his friend Dr. Franklin.

The popular story had it that Hillsborough was routed as a result of yet another anonymous, hilarious story in the press, "Rules by Which a Great Empire May Be Reduced to a Small One," a screed, written by Franklin, that was ostensibly directed to a statesman in power, kindly giving him advice. Hillsborough stepped down in August of 1772, whereas "Rules" did not appear in the *Public Advertiser* of London until September of the following year. It is possible, though, that the "Rules" were passed around in manuscript form among friends before they saw print, as was often done. It is also possible that Franklin had delayed their publication in the *Advertiser* in order to permit American journals to come forth with them at the same time, for he sent copies to America, as he had done with other, similar jokes. In any event, nobody doubted that it was to the Earl of Hillsborough that the "Rules" were addressed:

1. In the first place, gentlemen, you are to consider that a great empire, like a great cake, is most easily diminished at the edges. Turn your attention, therefore, first to your *remotest* province; that, as you get rid of them, the next may follow in order.

2. That the possibility of this separation may always exist, take special care the provinces are *never incorporated with the mother country;* that, as they do not enjoy the same common rights, the same privileges in commerce; and that they are governed by severer law, all of your enacting, without allowing them any share in the choice of the legislators. . . .

3. Those remote provinces have perhaps been acquired, purchased, or conquered, at the sole expense of the settlers, or their ancestors; without the aid of the mother country. If this should happen to increase her strength, by their growing numbers ready to join her wars; her commerce, by greater employment for her ships and seamen, they may probably suppose some merit in this, and that it entitles them to some favor; you are therefore to *forget it all, or resent it all,* as if they had done you injury.

It went on and on, unfailingly bland.

You are to suppose them *always inclined to revolt,* and treat them accordingly. Quarter troops among them. . . .

You ministers know that much of the strength of government depends on the opinion of the people, and much of that opinion on the *choice of rulers* placed immediately above them. . . . You are therefore to be careful whom you recommend to those offices. If you can find prodigals who have ruined their fortunes, broken gamesters or stock-jobbers, these may well do as governors. . . . Wrangling proctors and pettifogging lawyers, too, are not amiss. . . .

When such governors have crammed their coffers and made themselves so odious to the people that they can no longer remain among them with safety to their persons, *recall and reward* them with pensions. You may make them baronets too, if that respectable order should not see fit to resent it. . . . But remember to make your arbitrary tax more grievous to your provinces, by public declaration importing that your power of taxing them has *no limits;*

so that, when you take from them without their consent a shilling in the pound, you have a clear right to the other nineteen.

There are twenty articles in all, besides the preamble; and there is no doubt that the piece scored points for the colonies. But Samuel Adams still did not laugh.

CHAPTER EIGHTEEN

The Case of the Snickering Peers

It was the fall of 1771, according to his own account, when Adams first began to consider the possibility of joining all of the seacoast colonies into a union by means of committees of correspondence. "This is a sudden Thought and drops undigested from my pen," he wrote to Arthur Lee.

The South had only agriculture, which was not in competition with Great Britain, and indeed the British government was assisting certain sections of it—indigo farming, for instance. But the central and New England colonies depended in large part on their trade, and they aspired too, in order to alleviate the chronic shortage of cash, to establish their own manufactures.

The American merchants had many grievances. Their business was under all sorts of legal restraints. Vessels trading in or with the colonies had to be built in Great Britain, Ireland, the Channel Islands, or British colonies. All goods of European or oriental origin (tea, silks) must be imported from Great Britain, excepting Mediterranean salt, Madeira or Azores wine, and Irish horses, victuals, linen, and servants, which might be imported directly from the Emerald Isle.

The exports allowed to the American mainland colonies were in two classes, enumerated and nonenumerated, which meant all of the rest. The enumerated products, including tobacco, cotton, indigo, dyewoods, molasses, sugar, rice, coffee, pimiento, furs, hides and skins, naval stores, masts and spars, pot ash and pearl ash, whale fins, and iron, by far the greatest part of all that was produced in America, could be sent only to Great Britain, the British colonies, or, unexpectedly, West Africa. Wool yarns, woolens, and felt hats could not be exported at all, and could not even be sent to other American colonies. In addition, there were many onerous duties, bonds, cockets (customs-duty papers), and the like.

It was enough to drive a businessman mad, and the restrictions were being tightened all the time. No wonder the American merchants, though they sometimes feared that the Sons of Liberty were going too far, inclined in their direction.

The winter of 1771–1772 was a bad one for the Whigs, but soon afterward Adams was back promoting his earlier idea. "Let associations and combinations be everywhere set up to consult and recover our just rights," he was to write. He has been given full credit for the organization of the colonial committees of correspondence, and if this is more credit than any one man should get, he was certainly one of the first to propose them, as he was one of the most energetic to form them.

James Otis, in town for the last time, was made chairman of a House committee to consult on this matter. Otis himself did not think much of the committees-of-correspondence idea, but by that time he was no longer a force in Massachusetts politics and had been named to this chairmanship largely because the legislators felt sorry for him and wished to honor the memory of the man he had been.

Samuel Adams was secretary of this committee, and when it held its first meeting in the Town House on November 3, he had a report already written, which was adopted with only trifling changes.

The plan was a success from the beginning. Town after town in Massachusetts contributed, and soon whole colonies were coming in. Virginia, where both Patrick Henry and young Thomas Jefferson were strongly in favor of the plan, was especially diligent. Old enmities were not forgotten, but at least a start had been made toward cooperation.

Governor Hutchinson of Massachusetts was opposed to the plan, but there was nothing he could do but splutter. His popularity dropped lower every year. Nor was there any question of where he stood on the Tea Act; his own sons and his nephew were East India Company consignees.

There were always at least a few war vessels in Boston Bay these days. They were anchored innocently enough, it would seem, and for fear of desertion their crews were never granted shore leave. All the same, their cannons had big mouths. Yet it was not in Boston but in nearby Rhode Island that the first naval "incident" occurred.

Rhode Islanders took their smuggling seriously, and their resentment of anybody who tried to interfere with it could be sharp. When Lieutenant William Dudington, R.N., sailed into Narragansett Bay with H.M. schooner *Gaspée*, in March of 1772, he was marked for trouble right away. For this man believed that the laws ought to be enforced, and he strove to enforce them, stopping all sorts of vessels. He was chasing a craft early one evening near Providence when he went aground. It was impossible to float the schooner free until the high tide at midnight, and this gave the good people of Providence time to organize a party. They moved in a fleet of small boats. The *Gaspée* crew did not resist, but Dudington did, and accordingly he was shot. The schooner was burned.

Something similar had happened at about the same time in the lower Delaware, when men from the City of Brotherly Love seized a revenue vessel that had lately seized a smuggler, and took out of her all of the goods she had confiscated. This event, though bad enough, did not raise the stir that the *Gaspée* burning did. The Royal Navy created an extraordinary commission of admirals and governors to investigate the business, and dire threats were voiced. Unfortunately this commission, despite its distinguished makeup, could not find anybody who was able to identify the raiders. They had not worn masks or blacked their faces, but nobody in Providence could seem to name even one. The commission so noisily assembled got nowhere.

Then came the affair of the Whately letters, and all hope of reconciliation was ended.

Thomas Whately, who had died in 1772, was a member of the House of Commons and at one time a joint secretary of the treasury with George Grenville. He had corresponded with sundry Americans, and some of their replies got into the hands of Benjamin Franklin, who, seeking to prove to his new employers, the Massachusetts Assembly, that he was alive to their interests, mailed copies of these letters across the sea. He stipulated, as he did so, that they were not to be published.

The letters were from Thomas Hutchinson, Andrew Oliver, and a few now-forgotten minor officials. They were all personal. They expressed, of course, the Tory point of view, but there was nothing alarming in them. They were sixteen in number—six by Hutchinson alone—and not remarkable for literary merit.

It was not the letters themselves that caused Boston to seethe, but rather the manner of their publication. For they were eventually published, despite Franklin's provision.

At first the news was only hinted at. All the same, the hints were heavy, and when next the Assembly met, it was with a full attendance and with the gallery filled to the last seat. John Hancock, back in the Adams fold by this time, presided. He announced that he was about to read some interesting letters that lately had come from abroad. Samuel Adams here interrupted with the suggestion that the gallery be cleared and a guard posted outside the doors to prevent any interference on the part of the governor. This was done.

Adams himself read the letters. It must have been a masterful performance, for it infuriated the House.

Out-of-doors, people talked of little else. Bostonians were on fire to read those papers.

The governor was astounded. There was nothing in any of the letters that he had not said publicly again and again. There was nothing subversive or even unpatriotic. True, he decried the town meeting, which was the very heart and soul of the Massachusetts political system, but he decried it only as it was, to him, misused.

Copies of the letters, or extracts from them, were soon being circulated in Boston. A device was adopted that was so patent that it fooled nobody, but it did the trick. Hancock announced at the next meeting of the House that a man, whom he did not name, or perhaps did not know, had handed him a set of letters he said he had picked up on the Common. These letters, the speaker said, corresponded at a glance with those that had been sent from overseas.

It was then formally proposed that the secretary of the House, Mr. Adams, be instructed to compare the two sets of letters, and if they were in fact exactly alike, there was no reason why one set should not be published. Faith with Benjamin Franklin would thus be maintained, technically. This was done, and Samuel Adams, after a hasty examination, announced to no one's astonishment that the two sets of letters were indeed exactly alike. The House thereupon ordered that they be printed and distributed to the various committees of correspondence in Massachusetts and the other colonies.

First, the letters were "edited" by Samuel Adams and William Cooper, the latter having been Adams' chief assistant in the preparation of the late *Journal of Occurrences*. These men doctored the letters dexterously, often altering the meaning.

The result was the public damnation of Thomas Hutchinson, who was made to appear a plotter against his own country, a contriver of the Stamp Act as of the Tea Act, a partner in a plot to reduce Massachusetts to servitude.

Copies of the Adams-Cooper version of the letters were sent everywhere. The fact that they were only parts of private letters addressed to a private person (Whately had not been in office when they were sent and received) was not stressed. Indeed it was not even mentioned.

While indignation ran high, Samuel Adams presented the two houses of the General Court with a petition to the King, in which Hutchinson and Oliver were blamed for virtually everything that had gone wrong in Massachusetts since the end of the war, these two

having a natural & efficacious Tendency to interrupt & alienate the Affections of your Majesty our Rightful Sovereign from this your loyal province; to destroy that Harmony & Good Will between Great Britain and this Colony which every honest Subject would wish to establish; to excite the Resentment of the British Administration against this Province; to defeat the Endeavors of our Agents & Friends to serve us by a fair Representation of our State of facts; and to prevent our humble and repeated Petitions from reaching the Ear of your Majesty & having the desired Effect.

Finally, the petition requested that his Majesty "will be graciously pleased to remove them from their posts in this Government, and place such good and faithful men in their Stead as your Majesty in your great Wisdom shall think fit."

The motion was passed 111 to 28 in the Assembly and 15 to 5 in the Council.

Nobody expected that this petition would be granted, if it was even read. Its effect *locally* was what concerned the Patriots.

Lord Dartmouth did indeed take the petition to King George, who may have read it, and who referred it to His Majesty's Privy Council for Plantation Affairs. This body would of course reject the petition, but it occurred to somebody that the rejection should be done with a flourish, an example of fighting fire with fire.

Benjamin Franklin, who had come forward to admit that it was he who had sent the letters overseas, was the villain. The ministers were shocked to see private letters published— though for years they had been opening Franklin's own mail —and they were agreed that somebody must pay for this.

There had even been a duel fought about the Whately letters. William Whately, a London banker, brother of the late Thomas Whately, had been accused by John Temple, a government man, of selling the letters. He denied this hotly. The two had met with swords *and* pistols in Hyde Park, and Whately had been hurt and now was in a hospital. It was understood that the duel would be resumed as soon as Whately was up and around, and probably that is why Franklin came forward with his "confession."

The Council for Plantation Affairs called in as its lawyer Alexander Wedderburn, but the idea—the *only* idea—was to pillory Benjamin Franklin.

Wedderburn was a tall, sarcastic, mean-tempered young Scot who was working to get himself a title. He was an accepted past master of vituperation, a man with a tongue of Tabasco.

Lord Camden, who like everybody else knew what was about to happen, refused to attend the meeting, though he was a member of the council. Most of the members indeed were earls, or at least barons. Hillsborough was among them, North as well.

The chamber was crowded. Extra chairs had been brought in, and spectators were admitted, though this was not customary.

Benjamin Franklin was not offered a chair. He was sixty-eight years old, a distinguished scientist, but he was made to stand through all that followed, which lasted for almost an hour.

It was a one-man show. Wedderburn did not even make a pretense of considering the petition from the Massachusetts

General Court. That was not what he had been hired for. He simply stood there excoriating the doctor, who did not move, and who of course was not permitted to answer.

"Nothing then will acquit Dr. Franklin of the charge of obtaining them by fraudulent or corrupt means, for the most malignant of purposes; unless he stole them from the person who stole them. This argument is irrefragable."

The lords were amused, and they snickered, nudging one another with playful elbows. North alone stayed grave. The others teeheed like schoolboys.

"I hope, my lords, you will mark and brand this man, for the honour of this country, of Europe, and of mankind. . . . He has forfeited all the respect of societies and of men. Into what companies will he hereafter go with an unembarrassed face or the honest intrepidity of virtue?" asked this eminent lawyer. "Men will watch him with a jealous eye; they will hide their papers from him and lock up their escritoires."

There was more like this, much more. At last His Majesty's Privy Council for Plantation Affairs took a vote and decided unanimously to reject the petition.

The next morning Benjamin Franklin was notified that he was no longer postmaster general of His Majesty's American colonies, a position he had created and in which he had shone for many years. He started to pack.

Wedderburn got his title. He was created Baron Wedderburn of Loughborough.

CHAPTER NINETEEN

"That Bainfull Weed"

Just as no large-scale, centrally controlled Sons of Liberty organization existed, so those who called themselves the Daughters of Liberty had no officers to hold them together, no directors to lead them when once indignation started to wane. They were broken-up, come-and-go groups. The Sons could gird their loins whenever an alarm was sounded, and rush forth into the streets to do battle for the Lord, but the prime aim of the Daughters was a negative one—to abstain from drinking tea. Doggedly and courageously they had brewed raspberry leaves and dried thyme and pennyroyal, sassafras, and sage; they had also steeped catnip. Bravely they had referred to the real thing as "that nauseous concoction," and told one another that it could upset your stomach, could cause your hair to fall out, and, worse, was fattening. Still their efforts were in vain, and nowhere did the Daughters fail more shamefully than in New England.

Statistics compiled God knows how, and published widely throughout the colonies in 1773, had it that the port of Boston alone since the imposition of the Townshend duties had taken in more than three thousand chests of tea from England.

Until the emergence of tea as the central issue, the complaint of the rest of the colonies had been, generally, that Massachusetts was moving ahead too far too fast. Now it was the other way around. While Philadelphia, Charleston, and

New York were taking extraordinary precautions to prevent the landing of tea, Boston, it appeared, was doing nothing.

There were two reasons for this.

Boston did not have the smuggling facilities of most of the other colonies. The *tradition* was there, true. Many of the finest families had fortunes that were based on smuggling. But times change. The very vigor of the fight Massachusetts had led against all attempts to tax the colonies caused her to be marked out by the home country for special antismuggling treatment. Warships in Boston harbor were as thick as flies.

The second reason, which could be coupled with the first, was that the customs people in Massachusetts had hit upon this new idea of enforcing the laws. In New York or in Philadelphia it was relatively easy to bribe or to bully a tax collector. It was not so any longer in Boston.

Massachusetts, then, was behind the others, which made the others angry. For if the tea monopoly succeeded in one colony, it would succeed in all. No boycott works bit by bit.

From the beginning it had been patent to the Patriots that the best way to avert slavery-by-tea was to browbeat the men to whom the stuff was consigned, just as during the Stamp Act crisis they had successfully browbeaten the distributors-to-be. This worked in New York, in Philadelphia, in South Carolina, and in Maryland. It did not work in Massachusetts.

The consignees there were Richard Clarke & Sons, Thomas Hutchinson, Jr., Elisha Hutchinson, Benjamin Faneuil, and Joshua Winslow.

Richard Clarke was related to the governor by marriage. Elisha Hutchinson and Thomas Hutchinson, Jr., were the governor's sons. Jonathan Clarke was in England working to get the tea consignment. Isaac Clarke was out of town. Faneuil was a weak man who would do whatever the others said. Winslow was very old.

On November 5, a Friday, posters were put up all over

town instructing Bostonians to go to the Liberty Tree at the
junction of Newbury, Orange, and Essex streets, there to wit-
ness an affirmation on the part of sundry tea consignees that
they would not handle the stuff. Thus:

To the Freemen of this and the neighboring towns.
    GENTLEMEN,—You are desired to meet at Liberty Tree, this
day, at twelve o'clock at noon; and then and there to hear the persons to whom the tea shipped by the East-India Company is consigned, make a public resignation of their office as consignors upon
oath; and also swear that they will re-ship any teas that may be
consigned to them by said company by the first vessel sailing for
London.
    O.C., Secretary.
Boston, Nov. 5, 1773.
    ☞ Show us the man that dare take down this.

These consignees had been called upon at night by Sons of
Liberty, and told that they were to resign. They protested,
first, that they had not yet been commissioned to handle the
tea, and, second, that even if their papers of authority came
with the tea, as was likely, they themselves were bound by
whatever commitments their associates in England had made in
their name. They refused to give any promises.

In the morning the church bells rang for an hour, from
eleven o'clock until noon, but the crowd that gathered at the
Liberty Tree was disappointed. None of the consignees-
designate appeared.

Everybody knew where these men were. They were in the
Richard Clarke & Sons warehouse, a stout two-story wooden
building at the foot of King Street. The Patriots decided
to go there and visit them. A committee was appointed, and
its members marched down the middle of the street.

From a window of the Town House Governor Hutchinson
watched them go, and he marveled that there were many
among them who were not of the "lowest class." He himself

believed, and repeatedly had assured his superiors, that these lawless doings in Boston were wholly the work of the lowest classes.

At the warehouse no confrontation occurred, only a shouting back and forth through doors and walls. The consignees had barricaded themselves on the second floor. They refused an invitation to attend the meeting in "Liberty Hall," the outdoor space before the Tree. They called out that they would be willing to see the tea stored in a suitable place until they had received instructions from their employer-to-be, the East India Company. They would go no further than that.

The next day the same town meeting pronounced the consignees' answer "Daringly Affrontive to the Town," but that was all—for the present.

Some time since, all up and down the coast, men selected to sell the tea had been summoned before the Sons of Liberty and had pledged that on no account would they consent to receive it when it came.

On Wednesday, November 7, there sailed into Boston Bay John Hancock's fast brig *Hayley*, direct from London with a general cargo, no tea. Its skipper, James Scott, told the town elders that he had been approached by East India Company representatives to take on a full cargo of tea, but that he knew how his owner felt and had refused to handle the stuff. However, he said, there was a whole fleet of tea ships on its way. He had passed it in the Channel. Four of the vessels were headed for Boston, he said.

It was Boston that would tell the tale. Other places were waiting to see what she would do.

The law provided that, if duties on the cargo of a ship had not been paid within twenty days of that ship's arrival, the whole cargo must be sold at public auction. If that happened, it would be an opening wedge. It must not be permitted to happen.

Another part of this complicated law decreed that a taxable product, like tea, could not be sent back to the port from which it had come, on penalty of confiscation of both ship and cargo. The owners, then, would do everything that they could to prevent such a return voyage, assuming that the consignees remained adamant. But the owners might be forced.

Governor Hutchinson saw this, and it must be remembered that the governor believed a showdown was about to be called and that, if another concession was made to the Patriots, the whole power of the home country over the colonies would be dissipated. He ordered the admiral in charge of the naval forces in Boston Bay to arrange to fire upon any tea ship that might start to leave the harbor without having been unloaded.

Customarily a skipper was allowed forty-eight hours in which to report to customs, but it was not certain whether this could be taken into account in the forthcoming case. The law said that the duties must be paid "within twenty days after the first entry of the ship," but it did not define "first entry." Did it mean the actual entrance into the bay, or did it mean the "official" entrance—that is, the checking in at customs? If the latter, then perhaps the Patriots would have twenty-two rather than just twenty days, but with the customs force against them—not to mention the governor, the consignees, and the military—the Patriots could not take chances.

On Sunday, November 28, the bluff-bowed ship *Dartmouth* arrived, nine weeks out of London. She was carrying 114 chests of Bohea.

"The Tea that bainfull weed is arrived," Abigail Adams wrote to her friend Mercy Warren.

CHAPTER TWENTY

The Opalescent Windrows

The day was a Sunday, but the Board of Selectmen met anyway, so grave was the crisis. The *Dartmouth* reported at the customs house, and was then ordered (it is not clear by whom) to pull alongside of Griffin's Wharf.

Monday morning there were posters all over town, announcing a town meeting, though no such meeting had been legally advertised. Church bells were rung. Faneuil Hall was early filled to overflowing, and the session was moved to the Old South Church. It was estimated that there were five thousand persons there or trying to get in. Sheriff Greenleaf came and insisted upon reading a message from the governor, who declared that the meeting was an illegal one (as indeed it was) and ordered it dissolved. Greenleaf was booed, and he left.

A "watch" of twenty-five men was appointed to "protect" the *Dartmouth* and her cargo. These men immediately left for Griffin's Wharf. They were military about it, posting sentries and so forth.

The meeting at the Old South Church had adjourned until three o'clock. When it met again, it learned that Governor Hutchinson had issued an order to all justices of the peace to be on guard against tumults. The meeting denounced this as "an insult to the people of Boston," and then adjourned until the next morning.

While this was going on, the governor had called a special meeting of the provincial council, but that body did nothing. After the meeting the two Clarke sons and Benjamin Faneuil and Thomas Hutchinson, Jr., made their way to Castle William. It was not safe for them to stay in town overnight.

The governor was at his country place in Milton, eight or nine miles away; old Mr. Clarke was at Salem; the other Hutchinson son was visiting Andrew Oliver at Middleborough; Joshua Winslow was at Marshfield.

Next morning John Scollay, chairman of the Board of Selectmen, read to the again-seated Body the consignees' letter refusing to resign. The meeting began to discuss extreme measures. Twenty-three-year-old Francis Rotch, the son of Joseph Rotch of Dartmouth, Massachusetts, a rich whale-oil merchant, was rather harshly questioned—though no hand was laid upon him. The Rotch family, Quakers, owned the tea ship. Would they send her, complete with cargo, back? Young Rotch replied that they could not possibly do that, for confiscation would ruin them. What, he was asked, if the ship was *cleared* for England? If it was cleared by the governor himself, yes, replied Rotch. Whereupon he was sent off to Milton to see the governor.

It was awkward for the Patriots that the consignees were all rich men who had country houses, so that they were not always available. The artist John Singleton Copley, an in-law of the Clarkes, spoke up. A man not affiliated with either party, and trusted by both, he volunteered to go out to Castle William and confer with his relatives and their associates and see if he could not reach some solution. He was ordered to do this, and was given two hours.

Both missions failed. Copley was not able to persuade the consignees that they should resign from posts they had never held, while Governor Hutchinson believed that he had the Patriots right where he wanted them. The tea must be landed by December 17, or, properly, by midnight of the sixteenth, which would be a Thursday. If this was not done before the end of the twenty-day period, he, the governor, would be justified in calling out the redcoats to see that it *was*. As for giving clearance papers to the tea ship to enable it to return with its cargo to London, absolutely no, the governor said.

The ship *Eleanor* came in on December 2 and was tied up next to *Dartmouth*. The brig *Beaver*, which was also largely owned by the Rotch family, came a few days later, but she was carrying smallpox and had to be fumigated in a far corner of the bay. Therefore, she did not get in close until December 15, when she was anchored only a few yards away from the *Eleanor*.

The same "guard" watched over all three vessels. This group varied in number from twenty-four to thirty-six, and it was always there, day and night. The men did nothing to disturb the seamen, who came and went as they wished. Whether or not the guardsmen were armed was then and still is in dispute, but certainly at least they made no show of weapons.

Many of these Sons of Liberty were young, and some, to judge from the way they enjoyed keeping up a military routine, could have been Hancock's cadets. Hancock himself was sometimes seen among them for a short time, as though checking on their appearance.

The fourth tea ship, *William*, a brig, was wrecked on the ocean side of Cape Cod near Provincetown on December 10. Jonathan Clarke rode out of Castle William one dark night and managed to get a local sheriff to help him retrieve much of the tea, which was loaded aboard a fishing schooner that had been driven into Boston Bay by the same blow that had wrecked the *William*. This tea was stored in the fort. What eventually happened to it nobody knows.

Also aboard the *William* when she went ashore had been three hundred street lamps the town of Boston had recently bought in London. They too were salvaged, and were the first street lights that Boston ever had. The *William* itself was a complete loss.

The tea salvaged from the *William* was just a drop in the pot, a slip that did not in any way abash the Patriots. The real tea, the tea that must not be landed, was the tea in the *Dartmouth*, the *Eleanor*, and the *Beaver*. That was the tea that the men on Griffin's Wharf were "protecting."

It rained on December 16, the day of days. It rained pauselessly, implacably. The weather was cold too for that time of year. At the same time The Body was meeting again, or still, with Samuel Adams in the chair.

It must not be supposed that these meetings were the noisy gatherings of a revolutionary rabble. They were quiet, and carefully conducted according to parliamentary rules. There were no incendiary speeches, and nobody waved a cutlass or shouted for the severance of some tyrant's head.

Rotch was there again, a pale, plump, frightened young man. He was not interested in the tea, only in the vessels, *Dartmouth* and *Beaver*. His family stood to lose both of them if he was forced to send them back to England, unless of course the governor would issue clearance papers. The governor had refused to do this, but had countered with another suggestion—that the tea ships be worked out into the middle of the bay, there to be anchored under the guns of the various war vessels.

Rotch had said no to this suggestion. It would solve nothing, and would mean a long delay, at least until word of the predicament could reach London and the East India Company's reply could get back—three months, maybe longer. To the Rotches, time was money. They had use for the *Beaver* and the *Dartmouth*. A large supply of whale oil even then was on its way north to Boston, where it could be transferred to *Dartmouth* and *Beaver*, which would carry it to England.

Now The Body put it up to young Rotch again: Would

he go out to Milton once more and see what he could do? He consented.

The meeting stayed in session, but very little was done, and nothing important. Men talked in low tones. Now and then one would quit his place, but most of them stayed where they were, being afraid that if they left they would never get their seats back.

Late in the afternoon the rain stopped abruptly.

It was getting dark when Francis Rotch reappeared. The answer was negative. The governor would issue no clearance papers.

Samuel Adams spread his arms.

"This meeting can do nothing more to save the country!"

It was a signal. Men rose, whooping. Men cheered. They started for the door, while from the street came a hullabaloo. Samuel Adams, for all his quavering, managed to make himself heard as he pleaded for order, for a formal, proper adjournment. In time he got it, but thereafter, madness reigned.

So, at least, it seemed. In fact, everything was going according to schedule. The noise in the street was even greater than the noise inside, for other men were joining those who had not been able to get in, and these newcomers were yelling like Indians—or at least the way they thought Indians yelled. They were dressed appropriately. There were not many feathers in evidence, but each carried an ax or hatchet, which he waggled aloft like a tomahawk. No one was painted red, but the faces of all were daubed with something dark, in most cases lampblack, soot. They wore blankets or parts of blankets across their shoulders or tied around their waists. They greeted one another with "Ugh!" or with "How!" or more often with "Me know you," which seemed to be a sort of watchword.

There might have been twenty of these creatures, or thirty. Nobody counted. Besides, more were appearing all the time.

The crowd was fascinated, though probably not astonished.

The moon was up now, and it was a good clear night, and chilly. Everything gleamed with wetness.

When they had exchanged a sufficient number of welcoming grunts and "Me know you's," these improbable braves formed themselves in a double file. At a word of command from their sachems, or chiefs, they started to march down Milk Street.

A large part of what until a few minutes ago had been The Body trailed behind them. Some men, who lived nearby, ran to their homes to get lanterns. On either side of the "Indians," small boys skipped.

They turned into Hutchinson Street (Pearl Street now) and followed it down to where it crossed Flounder Lane.

Griffin's Wharf was a roofed building. The guards who had been posted there fell away before the newcomers, then closed ranks again, blocking the public from the wharf itself.

There was no need for the lanterns. The moon lighted everything.

Thousands witnessed the Boston Tea Party, which took about three hours, a little less. They were lined up along the waterfront. They were quiet, even thoughtful, watching.

There was nothing furtive about the business. The braves broke into three squads roughly equal in size, and some went to work in the *Dartmouth* whilst others climbed over the side-by-side gunwales to the *Eleanor*. The *Beaver* was worked alongside of the *Eleanor*, where she sogged into the mud, tipping a little. The other two vessels were already aground. It was low tide.

The captains, all three, were absent. The mates were there, however, and it was explained to them what was to be done. They made no protest.

Working on all three vessels at once, the Indians used the blocks-and-tackle they found there and the cranes. They hauled the tea up on deck and carefully smashed each chest. These were made of thin wood and gave them no trouble.

Inside, however, the tea was wrapped in tough burlap, which called for a more vigorous hacking. It was all carefully and thoroughly done, and the tea was dumped, loose, into the bay, where it floated in long lazy windrows opalescent in the moonlight. Little boys, wallowing gleefully in the mud under the wharf, pushed the piled tea off with brooms and boat hooks and sometimes barrel staves.

The clunk of axes was clear, crisp. It carried a long way. There was no other sound.

The Indians swept up afterward, leaving everything ship-shape. One padlock, the personal property of a skipper, was missing, and the redskins promised to replace it.

They lined up for a final inspection. They took off their blankets and their boots and shook the loose tea out of them, then swept it up and threw it into the bay. They marched off, keeping, as they had done when they came, a sort of rough order.

When the tide came in, the tea floated languidly out to the middle of the bay, where at last, soggy, it sank. There had been 342 chests of it, valued at £19,000.

Early the next morning somebody who didn't leave his name left a brand-new padlock aboard the *Dartmouth*.

CHAPTER TWENTY-ONE

The Cannons Had Big Mouths

Giving tea parties came to be a craze along the Atlantic Coast. The Sons in Philadelphia had made it clear what would happen to the Delaware River pilot who dared to guide a tea ship into that port. At Greenwich, New Jersey, the tea-carrying sloop *Greyhound* was burned to the waterline by another group of me-know-you Indians. Much the same thing occurred at Annapolis.

New York had a very tough Tory governor, William Tryon, and the pilots could not be terrified into compliance with the Sons of Liberty plans, for the governor had arranged for a warship to convoy the first tea ship in from Sandy Hook. But the New York Patriots solved this problem. A mob in the city so menaced that ship, when she was docked, that her skipper refused to order an unloading. A little later another tea ship was treated the same way the Boston braves had treated theirs: The tea was dumped into the bay.

Seven chests similarly were dumped into the Cooper River at Charleston, South Carolina, but this was only a sideshow. The main load, the first one, had been successfully brought ashore. However, there were no consignees to take possession of the tea in Charleston, these having been forced to resign in advance, and the stuff was stored in a damp warehouse, where much of it spoiled.

The *Grosvenor*, a brig, put in at Portsmouth, New Hampshire, with a varied cargo that included twenty-seven chests of tea, and the local Sons of Liberty saw to it that none of this cargo was landed. Boston even had a second tea party of its own. On Sunday afternoon, March 6, the brig *Fortune* brought in, among other things, twenty-eight and one half chests of tea. This shipment was not East India Company property but a private venture on the part of the skipper. The Sons talked it over with the customs people whilst *Fortune* lay alongside of Hubbard's Wharf, near Griffin's, but the Sons were not satisfied with whatever the officials offered, and sixty men garbed in the same so-called Mohawk costume soon boarded the *Fortune* and threw the tea over the rail.

Boston's first Tea Party attracted by far the most attention. The caper itself had been brilliantly brought off, the secret scrupulously kept, so that the "Indians" remained anonymous. The average Englishman, anyway, had come to regard Boston as the font and source of all American opposition to the Parliamentary taxation tactics. The East India Company had lost thousands as a result of the behavior of Sons of Liberty in other colonies, but still it was Boston, and Boston alone, upon which the whip of the ministry fell. The Royal Navy had noted that it might not be able to blockade a fifteen-hundred-mile coastline, but blockading one port would be easy. Moreover, the conviction was common that when Boston was smacked, the other colonies would all cry ouch.

It might be supposed that once the news of the Tea Party had reached Britain, the cry of *delenda est Carthago* would be loud in the land. It was heard, indeed, but not often at first. Many of the English took it for granted that the East India Company would get not only full reparations but an apology. Some chuckled, appreciating the sportiness of the Tea Party, but even they assumed that, as soon as the mess could be cleaned up, Bostonians would be made to pay in hard cash for their temerity.

The English merchants never lost sight of the £4 million that American businessmen owed them, and most likely the Americans were not forgetting it either. Many *non*mercantile friends of America in England, some of them themselves Americans, counseled a prompt and unquestioning repayment. One such was Benjamin Franklin, who just at that time was packing his things to go. When Samuel Adams learned of this, he remarked grumpily that Dr. Franklin might be a fine scientist and a fine philosopher, but he didn't know his politics.

In America it was generally assumed that retribution would be swift and probably harsh. After all, the Tea Party had been an overt act.

In England opinion was divided. The first question asked, "Why did they do it?" did not give birth to many echoes. People had come to expect almost anything of those wild Bostonians. The question that soon followed, "How should they be punished for it?" caused a great deal more fuss. Unexpectedly it turned out that there were some few who thought that they should not be punished at all. America, it seemed, had a great many more friends in England than anybody until this time had supposed. There was a decided outcry, in the press and elsewhere, to go easy on the Bostonians, to forgive them, for they knew not what they did.

The cabinet ministers were not a part of this faction. They pondered. They asked Edward Thurlow, the attorney general, and the solicitor general, Lord Loughborough, what *they* thought of the situation legally. The reply was that there existed "an open rebellion and war in the Province of Massachusetts Bay," after which triumph of logical deduction the ministers grimly announced their decision. It was fourfold:

1. The port of Boston was closed. After June 1, 1774, no vessel could enter the harbor, and after June 15 none could leave. The seat of the Massachusetts government was moved to Salem. The customs house was moved to Plymouth. This, which was done in the name of the King, would last *at least*

until the East India Company had been fully repaid for the loss of the tea.

2. The Administration of Justice Act was designed to protect the customs man who, while trying to do his duty, was arrested on a capital charge. It provided that he should be tried not in the colony in which he was arrested but in another colony or (and this seemed more likely) England.

3. The Massachusetts Government Act for all practical purposes abrogated that colony's charter. It provided that members of the Council should be appointed by the King's representative, the governor, rather than by members of the lower house of the General Court. The governor was also authorized to appoint inferior court judges and court officials and some county officials as well, including sheriffs, who would pick juries. Only one town meeting a year was to be permitted, and it must confine itself to local business.

4. The Quartering Act was extended. It applied to all of the colonies, not just to Massachusetts, but it had obviously been inspired by the behavior of Boston. It provided that the commander in chief of the military forces in America could press into service any unoccupied barns, stables, warehouses, or other buildings as barracks for his men at any time he saw fit.

These laws, collectively, were known in England as the Coercive Acts. Americans called them the Intolerable Acts.

They were all bad, but the first was the worst. It eliminated Boston's whole *raison d'être*, for a port that is no longer a port is nothing, and Boston, just as it was faced with a £19,000 bill for damages, was deprived of its only means of making money. Not only was traffic with the home country prohibited, and traffic with Europe, with the West Indies, everywhere, but even coastwise shipping was to be denied to rebellious Boston.

Salem and Plymouth scorned to take advantage of the business that had been thrust upon them and immediately offered to send to Boston whatever the stranded town needed.

However, this could not be done by boat, for all water-borne traffic was forbidden, but only by wagon train over long, crooked, back-straining roads. Even the Charlestown ferry, a scant half-mile hop, was banned.

Moreover, this had been done all at once, and without any warning, without a hearing. In London, William Bollan, the lawyer for the Massachusetts Council, prepared a statement that he asked the House of Commons to permit him to read; but this was denied. Bollan did, a little later, too late, get a hearing in the House of Lords, but the petition got up by thirty-odd Americans resident in England, headed by Franklin's successor, Arthur Lee, was not admitted to either house.

How did all this happen? Granted that it was a low period in British political history, a time of all minnows and no whales; granted that three thousand miles allowed room for a great deal of leakage; still, were there not *some* members of Parliament who would oppose this act of monumental stupidity?

Some thought that Boston should at least be given a hearing, but they were outnumbered by the angry ones who cried that there had been too many hearings already. It was said, now, that the Stamp Act never should have been repealed. You simply couldn't please those brash Americans.

Many who voted for the Boston Port Bill would have refused to do so if they had known how the thing was packaged. Lord North was a master parliamentarian, and he produced his restraining bills one by one, keeping those to come a secret until the one on hand had been passed. The whole corrosive program came as a shock to many M.P.'s who had been coaxed into consenting to it bit by bit.

Thus, the enactments that followed the Port Act, clinching it, slipped quietly into place, a little at a time, but they were to hit America all at once, causing consternation.

Many members of Parliament looked upon the Port Bill as a temporary emergency measure, for the assumption seemed to be general that Boston would pay for the tea and apologize—promptly. It never occurred to the M.P.'s that Boston might resist. Moreover, the belief was widespread in Britain that Massachusetts would be deserted by its friends. The American colonies inevitably would quarrel over the matter, and pull apart.

But Boston was *not* left alone. Other colonies rushed to her assistance with resolutions of approval and injunctions to stand fast. To keep Bostonians from starving, two shiploads of rice came from faraway South Carolina, getting there before the Port Bill went into effect. Philadelphia sent a thousand barrels of flour, Wethersfield, Connecticut, a thousand bushels of grain. Herds of cattle and droves of pigs were shooed in from nearby communities, and fresh vegetables were brought, also firewood, and when a purse was raised in Fairfax County, Virginia, for the suffering Bostonians, Colonel George Washington, never a man to give money away carelessly, was one of the first subscribers, putting himself down for £50.

The situation was confusing, but one thing at least was sure: The Americans were going to stick together.

CHAPTER TWENTY-TWO

The Lawn Sleeves Controversy

In a companion, stupidity is embarrassing. In a statesman, it's a sin. Those who so spectacularly misguided the British Empire when it was young, then, were sinners. The mass of them had no imagination, and they submitted without demur to a rotten system.

Ah, but look at Pitt! cry some. Well, look at him. He was a leader whom nobody followed, a stage actor so bedazzled by his own brilliance as to be, in effect, blind. If he sometimes *seemed* great, it was because of the company that he, perforce, kept. In truth he was like Swift's Emperor of the Lilliputians, who "is taller by almost the breadth of my nail than any of his court, which alone is enough to strike an awe into the beholders." William Pitt scintillated, but to what purpose? He sent out words as bright as skyrockets; they blazed for a moment, then fell, black and burned out.

The Great Commoner did win the Seven Years' War, though some have noted that he did it with the help of the British Army as well as the Royal Navy. He did not win the peace. The war was taken away from him just as the drums were sounding their conquering roll. This saved his reputation. The peacemakers who squeezed so much out of a defeated France, solidifying the bitterness that was left and making another world conflict inevitable, would have squeezed even more if William Pitt had been among them. By his own admission, he believed that they had been too compassionate.

The one shining sample of statesmanship that this clique of politicians *did* sponsor was the Quebec Act of 1774. Pitt, Lord Chatham now, hotly opposed the Quebec Act. When it came up in the Lords, he held forth against it for two hours, leaving the other peers exhausted after such exposure to the celebrated eloquence. Nevertheless, they were still able to summon the strength to vote 3½ to 1 for the bill, which had barely squeezed through the Commons.

The Quebec Act was not a sudden thing. It had been thought out, and for a long while. There were four separate drafts of it before it went to Parliament.

James Wolfe, had he not got himself killed, undoubtedly would have been made the military governor of conquered Canada, and undoubtedly, too, he would have been a very poor governor, for he was narrow-minded, unstable, emotional, and erratic. His successors, Amherst and Carleton, who were also full-time soldiers, and dedicated generals, faced up realistically to the problem of what should be done about Canada. Indeed, their original recommendations formed the basis of the Quebec Act.

In England, where there persisted memories of Bloody Mary and the Smithfield fires, of Guy Fawkes and the Gunpowder Plot, Roman Catholics were not permitted to hold office or to have commissions in the armed services. Such restrictions could not be imposed upon Canada (which was then called, collectively, Quebec), because Catholics there outnumbered the Protestants 350 to 1. Moreover, the Canadians were all French and virtually all of them were illiterate. The framers of the Quebec Act were not unaware of the way the French missionaries had stirred up the ignorant Indians, in some cases causing them to believe that the Virgin Mary had been born in Paris and Jesus crucified in London. The Jesuits were ruled out of Canada under the new dispensation, but the tithes were retained, and the Roman Catholic Church was recognized.

Canadians had been accustomed to tyranny for so long that they were not much concerned with the way the King's minions ran things in London—they had made no squawk at the Stamp Act—but they could not be expected all of a sudden to embrace democracy and make it work. The Quebec Act provided for no Canadian legislature, but only for a council, the members of which would be appointed by a crown-appointed governor. More, it substituted French law for English law in all *civil* cases, though in *criminal* cases English law prevailed. This led to a cry, on both sides of the sea, that the principle of trial by jury was being thrown out, which was only partly true.

Such English and Scottish merchants as had moved to Canada since the war were there for what they could get, and they were furious when the passage of the Quebec Act made them politically what in fact they had always been—a tiny minority. Some of them one night blackened a heroic bust of George III in a public place in Montreal, hanging around its neck a sign that read: "The Pope of Canada and the fool of England."

That the Quebec Act was wise, that it was foresighted, liberal, and realistic has been generally conceded, but its proposal in Parliament raised a storm. To an even greater extent it shocked English-speaking America, where men fairly screamed.

The Quebec Act was not and never had been one of the Coercive Acts. It was written by different men. The arguments advanced in its favor were totally unlike the arguments for the Coercive or Intolerable acts. Nevertheless, and in part because the news of it came at the same time, it was accepted in America as one of the supports of the Boston Port Bill. Many American leaders who were otherwise well informed were to believe this to their dying day. The Quebec Act *must* be a part of the grand movement to stamp out all colonial rights. The loudest of all who cried havoc was

Samuel Adams of Purchase Street. He had written, only a few years before, in the *Gazette:*

I did verily believe, and I do so still, that much more is to be dreaded from the growth of POPERY in America, than from the Stamp-Acts or *any other* Acts destructive of mens *civil* rights: Nay, I could not help fancying that the Stamp-Act itself was contrived with a design only to inure the people to the habit of contemplating themselves as the slaves of men; and the transition from thence to a subjection to Satan, is mighty easy.

Such a novelty as a colonial administration bill that showed some respect for the background of the colonists was bound to attract attention. In England the distaste for it was based largely on legal grounds, while in America it was territorial. What sort of way is that to found an empire, by throwing away the dearest Anglo-Saxon privilege of them all, the right of trial by jury? the English cried. What sort of way is that to betray your loyal subjects, by surrounding them with minions of the papacy? the New Englanders wailed.

In the minds of many the Quebec Bill and its abhorrent freeing of the Catholics was tied up with what men in those days called the Lawn Sleeves Controversy.

The British colonies in America were in the see of the Bishop of London, nobody knew why. No bishop had ever visited them, and when the Anglican Church did begin to pay attention, early in the eighteenth century, it took the form of the Society for Propagating the Gospel in Foreign Parts. The SPG was started in London in 1701, and its condescending title alone would have made Americans dislike it. Who *needed* to have the Gospel propagated to them? Sturdy old New Englanders in particular, men whose ancestors had crossed the sea precisely in order to get rid of bishops and incense and all the rest of the Roman frills, knew their Gospel backward and forward, and could quote it by the yard—and frequently did.

The Society, for all of its pretensions, did little about the Indian and even less about the Negro. The planters, both in the West Indies and in the mainland South, did not like anybody meddling with the Negroes. Yet the SPG seemed set upon establishing itself in America, and for this purpose it needed a bishop of its own.

Most of the colonial governors, being appointees of the crown, were Episcopalians, and their households were little courts. This gave the Church of England in America a snob appeal of which the SPG was quick to take advantage. But a bishop was a peer of the realm, with a seat in the House of Lords. Also, he was expensive.

Samuel Adams considered bishops to be "knobs and wens and bunchy popish flesh," and this opinion was shared by many in America. Even Virginia, where the Church of England was officially established, shied in alarm at any mention of an American bishop. Bishops represented authority. They represented pomp, repression, taxes.

The SPG had many enemies, and it was often slandered, but its eagerness to have an American see was natural enough. Without a bishop how could the Church continue to exist in America, much less expand?

There was never a time between the founding of Jamestown and the outbreak of the Revolution when some sort of bishops-are-coming rumor did not swirl through the colonies. Some were scare stories pure and simple, but others were based on fact, for several times the thing really was near. A great deal depended upon the monarch of the moment. The last two Stuart kings, Charles II and his brother, James II, a Catholic, at no time were interested in the enlargement of the Church of England, but one of their successors, Anne, decidedly *was*. The first two Georges accepted the Church of England as a duty imposed upon them, a royal obligation. Their motto might have been *Cuius regio eius religio*. But now George III, a devout Anglican, was on the throne, and again it seemed there was a good chance that an American bishopric might be created. With the passage of the Quebec Act this fear was intensified.

The two things were not in any way connected, but each aroused, and at the same time, the anti-Catholic and anti-Establishmentarian feelings of Americans, in whose minds they became one.

Finally, those Americans who were not wrought up about the Catholic provisions of the Quebec Act were furious about the geographical ones. For the bill stipulated that "Quebec" should be made to include not only all of the Canadian territories but also, arbitrarily, the lands west of the Alleghenies, north of the Ohio, east of the Mississippi, all of what was then called the Northwest Territory—today's Ohio, Illinois, Michigan, Indiana, and Wisconsin. Here again the motives of the bill's framers were laudable. They wished to protect the Indians by making the Northwest Territory crown land. This would prevent the encroachment of settlers from the seacoast colonies, who, once they had crossed the mountains, would be sure to swindle the Indians out of their acreage. The framers of the Quebec Act knew that the Indians in those parts were not an agricultural people but hunters. They needed a lot of land or they could not live. Hemmed in, they would explode.

What the framers did not seem to want to acknowledge was that the coastal colonists had already for some time been pushing forward into this territory, while even the ones who stayed at home were investing in those lands, sight unseen, without asking the inhabitants' permission. Speculation in such lands was rife, and some of the investors were prominent and influential men. To such as these the British gave a Canutelike command: Stay out.

The Quebec Act was farseeing, a model piece of legislation, an example of the way a mother country should treat its children. All that was wrong with it—and this was vital—was the timing. Those ministers! The one good thing that they had done was done badly.

CHAPTER TWENTY-THREE

The Cantankerous Bostonians

It is said that if two persons love one another long enough and with sufficient fervency, they will come to look alike. It has never been said that this will happen if two persons *hate* one another. Yet undeniably there was a distinct resemblance, in both body and face, between Samuel Adams and the governor of Massachusetts.

This was not Governor Shirley, the wartime executive, who had lately gone to his reward, nor yet Governor Pownall, who had retired and now lived in London. It was not Governor Bernard, back in England, a country gentleman, nor was it Anne Hutchinson's distinguished descendant Thomas. Adams had feuded with all of these, for he instinctively dashed at a governor as any knight of old might dash at a dragon. It was Lieutenant General Thomas Gage, commander in chief of his majesty's military forces in America. Copley, who had painted both Gage and Adams, remarked upon the likeness.

Gage was a mannerly man. He did not glitter, and his rise had been steady if unspectacular. He had seen action at Fontenoy and Culloden and in the Low Countries, also under Braddock at the wilderness catastrophe of July 9, 1755, from which fracas he had escaped with only a small wound. It was there that he had met George Washington, whom he liked. Soon afterward Gage, a full colonel now, participated in another large-scale defeat, Abercromby's failure to take Ticonderoga. He served under Amherst, a hard man to please. He was married to the former Margaret Kemble of Brunswick, New Jersey, a lady tall, willowy, and productive; they had many children.

All of Thomas Gage's adult life had been spent in the army, and virtually all of it in the colonies.

He was a careful man. He liked to compromise whenever compromise was possible, but he believed that when force was needed, it should be applied promptly and thoroughly. As commander in chief he kept his headquarters in New York, where he and his wife maintained a large and rather dowdy house in Broad Street.

Gage had lately been on leave in England, where he was much questioned about the situation in the colonies. The King liked him; "my gentle general," he called him.

Thomas Hutchinson, a devil to the radicals, by his brusqueness and his stubbornness had lost the faith of many of the American Tories as well. Therefore, it was decided in England that under the Coercive Acts, Massachusetts should have a military man as governor, though it was not, at least at first, to be under military rule. The gentle general was sent.

He arrived in Boston on May 13, 1774, and spent four days at Castle William before going into town. He had ordered up four more regiments—the 4th, 5th, 38th, and 43rd infantry, besides three companies of artillery—and they were already on their way.

Thomas Hutchinson left Boston—forever, as it proved—on June 1. The departure was not a gala occasion. It was, by chance, the very day when the Port Bill went into effect, and Boston was draped in mourning, with flags at half-mast, and church bells tolling dolefully. A bitter man, Hutchinson believed that he had been betrayed by his own countrymen. He was never to see his beloved Milton again, but would die in England and be buried there.

The men at Whitehall and Windsor had been impressed by

Gage's quiet confidence in his ability to quell the Massachusetts pothers. He still exuded this confidence at the welcoming banquet, when everything seemed rosy, but it began
to seep out of him soon afterward. The Bostonians were a
cantankerous lot. They called a town meeting, and when Gage
reminded them that it was forbidden now, they pointed out
that this one was an *adjourned* meeting. A thing like that, Gage
protested, could be kept up for years. They agreed.

Though there were a few rich merchants who offered to
contribute to a fund for the payment of the tea, the town
meeting refused even to discuss the matter. General Gage did
not have the authority to abrogate the Boston Port Bill, and
even if he had, it would have taken at least three months for
the word to get to London and then back to him. By that time
an unassisted Boston would have been no more than a ghost
town. Already, and even with supplies arriving from the other
colonies, coming in huge lumbering wagons across the Neck
—"Lord North's Coasters," the colonists called them (Boston
even had to get its codfish this way)—the streets were filled
with unemployed men.

When the governor at last did succeed in suppressing town
meetings, the colonists simply held *county* meetings instead.
There was no law against county meetings, they pointed out.

Gage was easy to meet; he would receive any committee
or delegation, or any individual with a legitimate complaint,
and listen to them long and carefully. Among his own followers he maintained the strictest discipline, and the redcoats,
as before, had to take whatever the townspeople threw at them,
making no reply.

The redcoats were everywhere now. Gage arranged to
build barracks right in the center of town, and he fortified the
Neck, so that Boston became more than ever like a besieged
place. In London much hope had been placed on the new plan
to make the council a part of the General Court appointive
by the governor, whereas previously the councillors had been

named by the Assembly. Gage, however, had a hard time *getting* a council. Man after man refused to accept this honor with the Sons of Liberty lurking in the background. When Gage did at last get such a group, it was a sad one, a scared one.

The lieutenant governor should have been the chairman or leader of the council. The lieutenant governor at this time was Thomas Oliver. He had recently succeeded his brother Andrew, who had resigned because of ill health. Now Thomas too resigned. He had been cornered in Cambridge by a group of the Sons, and they had talked to him.

The radicals still were in control. The very day on which the news of the Boston Port Bill was received, May 10, 1774, had been a General Court election day. Out of the 536 votes cast in Boston, Thomas Cushing and William Phillips got enormous majorities in their districts, while John Hancock got *all* of the votes in his, and Samuel Adams all but one in his.

All up and down the coast other bodies, as colonies or as towns or counties, were passing resolutions deploring the Boston Port Bill, which they took to be directed against them as much as it was directed against Boston, and pledging themselves not to import British goods until it had been repealed. Gage, however, had all he could handle right in Massachusetts. There, as elsewhere, a Solemn League and Covenant was being circulated, pledging the signers to nonimportation.

There was also abroad a movement for the calling of a Continental Congress. The suggestion had been made by New York and endorsed by the many committees of correspondence in Virginia, Massachusetts, and elsewhere. Philadelphia actually had sent out an invitation, it being the logical place for such an assembly, both because of its central location and because of its rooming-house accommodations. When Governor Gage learned that the lower house of the Massachusetts General Court was about to endorse this plan and to name delegates, he went into action.

He had called a session of the assembly for June 17. It was to be held in Salem, no longer in Cambridge, which nobody had liked. Not many members liked Salem either, but that was the place where the men in London thought it ought to be. Gage himself went to Salem, to keep his eye on the session.

They were in secret session, but he had his spies, and he heard of what was going on. Hastily he wrote an executive order dissolving the assembly, and he sent the provincial secretary, Thomas Flucker, to read the order to the offenders.

The Patriots too had spies. Flucker found the chamber locked. He pounded on the door for a little while, and then he read the order aloud to those few who had gathered on the steps outside, and he left.

The doors were opened. The plan for a Continental Congress had been warmly endorsed, and a delegation of five was appointed. One of them, of course, was Samuel Adams.

Thomas Gage, bewildered by this behavior, did what every general always does when he is bewildered. He sent for reinforcements.

CHAPTER TWENTY-FOUR

The Die Is Cast

A coach, like a sword, like a scepter, was a symbol. It was a symbol of power. Governors rode in coaches, and so did very rich men. The delegates to the First Continental Congress from Massachusetts had a coach.

Oliver Cromwell had locked his Parliament out. Samuel Adams locked his *in*. When he fastened the door of the chamber that housed the last Massachusetts General Court assembly in Salem, Adams put the key into his pocket and resumed the chair. It was his intent not only to keep out any representative of the governor but also to keep in any Tory members who might think to tell Governor Gage what was going on. One such Tory had got out beforehand, on a plea of illness, but that was the only hitch in Adams' schedule; everything else went off as planned. Not only did he, in the scant time allowed him, read the invitation from the Philadelphia Patriots, but he also submitted a resolution calling for the endorsement of the Congress plan and the appointment of a slate of five delegates, having arranged for prompt seconders for each of these names. Adams had even thought to call for and get an appropriation of £500 for the delegates' expenses. Why shouldn't they hire a coach?

It was the dignity of the province that they were thinking of, not their own. The coach might be majestic, but it was damned uncomfortable. They planned to use it only when they entered or left some considerable town. Between such places they meant to exercise their legs by walking, or else to ride the led horses.

One delegate, James Bowdoin, was not there when they met at Thomas Cushing's house for the takeoff on August 10; his wife was ill, and he would join them later. In the springless coach, then, when it left Boston, there were "a brace of Adamses," and Cushing and Robert Treat Paine. In front of them were two white outriders, behind them four Negroes, two mounted, two on foot. It made quite a procession. They were careful to ride past the Common, so that the encamped redcoats could see them.

It is assumed that Cushing and Paine and the Braintree Adams were wearing their very best clothes. It is *known* that Samuel Adams was wearing his. Even the grandeur of the coach would be diminished if there were to emerge from it the usual Samuel Adams in his faded and much-patched apparel. His friends, realizing this, had staged one of those quiet present-giving parties, one visitor casually leaving half a dozen pairs of stockings, another as though absentmindedly a couple of shirts, still another a new coat or a pair of shoes.

He might have been uneasy even if it had not been for the finery, for in all his life before he had never been more than a few miles from Boston. Now he was about to go out into the world.

Watertown was their first stop, and there they were made much of. After Watertown it was proposed that a couple of them use the led horses, for the coach was cruel on their behinds. Naturally the senior, Samuel Adams—he was fifty-two —was offered first choice. He declined, for an extraordinary reason. He didn't know how to ride a horse. He had never had time to learn.

So Samuel Adams thudded the whole distance in that lumbrous vehicle, which must have been torture. His cousin John, who was learning this about him for the first time, vowed that when they got to Philadelphia he would see that Samuel took riding lessons. He needed the exercise anyway, John said.

Providence, New London, Lyme, New Haven—at each town there was a new committee of welcome, a new inn, a new meal, and the same old exuberant toasts. Local cadets were lined up in their honor; selectmen handed them scrolls; field-pieces were fired.

They spent four days in New York, putting up at Mr. Hull's Bunch of Grapes, and then, after a ferry trip, the thudding was resumed, across New Jersey this time. At Princeton, on August 27, they paused for a long consultation with the president of New Jersey College, the gnarled, tart Dr. Witherspoon, a dedicated Patriot.

They crossed the Delaware at Trenton. Several miles outside Philadelphia they were met by an informal committee of advisers, and over a tavern table they were earnestly cautioned not to act *too* Down Eastern when they did reach the City of Brotherly Love. The Southern delegates, and those from the middle colonies as well, they were warned, were leery of New Englanders, especially those from Massachusetts, and *most* especially of Samuel Adams, who was believed to be an irresponsible fire-eater. Did they understand? They bowed their heads gravely and humbly, saying that yes, they did understand, and they would bear it in mind, thanks.

Arrived at journey's end, they were put up in the rooming house of Miss Jane Port in Arch Street.

The First Continental Congress was many things, but first of all it was an extralegal meeting of minds. Its very existence was a challenge to the authority of Parliament and King. It was no crowd of jabbering revolutionaries! It was rather an assemblage of sober men who were as unsure of one another—most of them were meeting for the first time—as they were of the effect that their getting together would have upon the rest of the world.

Not all of the delegates could be rated as radicals, like the

Virginians, like the men from Massachusetts. Many were of the mercantile persuasion, or represented mercantile interests, especially those from the powerful colonies of New York and Pennsylvania. Leading the conservatives, men determined at all costs to save the tie with England, was Joseph Galloway, a Philadelphia lawyer of awesome talents. Galloway, like so many others, for a long time had been watching from afar, and with mixed admiration, the doings of Samuel Adams, who would of course be his chief opponent. Now, meeting Adams in the flesh, Galloway found him "a man who, though by no means remarkable for brilliant abilities, yet is equal to most men in popular intrigue and the management of a faction." Galloway noted that "he eats little, drinks little, sleeps little, thinks much, and is most decisive and indefatigable in the pursuit of his objects."

Galloway sprang his own plan upon the visiting delegates almost before they had settled in their seats.

Twelve of the thirteen colonies were represented. The thirteenth was Georgia, the least populous and the farthest away, which in any event would have almost certainly done as the Carolinas did.

Galloway admittedly was no innovator when he proposed a colonial union that would remain within the British Empire, a prototype of the Commonwealth Plan. His proposal, if adopted, and if agreed upon by the mother country, would have greatly changed the course of history. It would also have knocked Samuel Adams' plans into a cocked hat.

The Galloway plan was admirably brief. To start, it struck a popular note:

Resolved, That this Congress will apply to His Majesty for a redress of grievances, under which his faithful subjects in America labour, and assure him that the colonies hold in abhorrence the idea of being considered independent communities on the British Government, and most ardently desire the establishment of a political union, not only among themselves, but with the mother state.

This should consist of "a President General, to be appointed by the King, and a grand council to be chosen by the Representatives of the people of the several colonies in their respective assemblies, once in every three years." The President General would serve during the pleasure of the King, and he would have an absolute veto over the enactments of the council, a veto from which there could be no appeal.

Galloway very nearly made it. Under the rules that this extraordinary body had made for its own conduct, each colony, whether large or small, and no matter how many delegates represented it, had but one vote. One delegation, North Carolina, was absent at the time of the vote. The others voted against the Galloway resolution, 6 to 5.

The Adamses breathed again.

The previous night a middle-aged Boston silversmith named Paul Revere, a prodigiously durable horseman, had ridden into Philadelphia with a set of resolutions just passed by the Suffolk County, Massachusetts, *county* meeting. The Adamses placed them before the Continental Congress.

Samuel Adams had not written the Suffolk Resolves, but undoubtedly he knew, when he set forth from Philadelphia, what they would contain, for he had left instructions concerning them.

There had been several "early" declarations of independence, pre-July 4, 1776, papers, including the Mecklenburg Declaration of North Carolina and the Virginia Stamp Act Resolutions of May 30, 1765. However, the Suffolk Resolves, as adopted by Samuel Adams' Boston town meeting, which moved first to Dedham, then to Milton, were the loudest, the clearest, and the best.

They were not the best *written*—the real penmen of the Revolution, Samuel Adams and Thomas Jefferson, would have used less bombast and fewer words altogether—but they made their point.

They urged Americans to "use their utmost diligence to acquaint themselves with the art of war as soon as possible." They pledged nonimportation; they encouraged the establishment of manufactures; they declared that any attempt to apprehend and transport for trial "sundry persons of this county who have rendered themselves conspicuous in contending for the violated rights and liberties of their countrymen" should be blocked by force; and they called for the convening of a provincial congress, "to be holden at Concord, on the second Tuesday of October next ensuing." They virtually declared war.

The Continental Congress, having rejected the Galloway Plan, endorsed in full the Suffolk Resolves.

The die had been cast.

CHAPTER TWENTY-FIVE

Touchy, Touchy

Thomas Gage was puzzled. Nothing had turned out the way he planned. It had all seemed easy in England when he explained it to His Majesty, but in the field the opposition refused to obey the rules, and the situation was getting worse every day.

To defend Boston would have been easy. A handful of regulars behind the barricade on Boston Neck could have held off hordes of colonials, while the water by which the town was virtually surrounded was his, the Bostonians not being permitted so much as a rowboat. But—why defend Boston? Boston wasn't America. There were few Patriots left there now, and more Tories kept coming in all the time from the countryside, while radical leaders slipped out.

It was not Boston that the governor worried about; it was the hinterland. He had his spies, and what he learned was disconcerting. The Massachusetts militia, until the other day just a joke but now in every town and village, was meeting not merely once or twice a year but once or twice a *week*, and was drilling assiduously. Moreover, it was storing supplies, in caches well back from the coast. It was gathering powder and lead, flour too, and when it did not have enough of its own, it didn't hesitate to raid the King's stores in seaport towns. Gage would have liked to send out troops to seize these stores himself, but every time a small body of redcoats ventured beyond Boston Neck, it was followed by watchful militiamen. This could lead to a flare-up, so Gage refrained.

"I think it would be policy to temporize a while by suspending the execution of the [Intolerable] Acts for a time and the province might send home Deputies and in the meanwhile to prepare for the worst," he wrote to ex-Governor Hutchinson on September 17, 1774. "Hanoverians and Hessians may be hired and other steps taken necessary to ensure success for by all appearances these provinces must be first totally subdued before they will obey and a powerful force must in that case be employed."

Late in September and early in October his reinforcements began to arrive, the 10th and 52nd from New York, the 18th and 47th from Newfoundland, besides two companies of the 65th, together with 400 marines the Navy lent him. Boston was getting badly crowded. But even with all these men Gage had only about 3,500 useful troops under his immediate command, though he had told the ministry again and again that he needed at least 20,000.

Partly in order to exercise his troops, partly in order to get them used to the countryside of eastern Massachusetts and to cause the people therein to become used to *them*, Gage began sending out small parties, a hundred or fewer, on all-day hikes. Under stern orders, they minded their own business, but skeptical militiamen were always there to watch them.

Nobody ever questioned General Gage's personal courage, but he was not a bold man, and now, near the end of his career, he was convinced that London did not appreciate the touchiness of the situation. He believed with all his heart in the supremacy of Parliament, but he also believed that the Americans, if pressed, would fight.

Both officially and unofficially in letters to England he urged that the Navy be used to establish a blockade. If this was done, however, he did not wish to see any considerable body of troops left in the colonies, at least not until complete submission had been made. The Navy could do the job best, he, an Army man, believed.

Above all, he counseled firmness. "If you think ten Thousand Men sufficient, send Twenty, if one Million is thought enough, give two; you will save both Blood and Treasure in the End. A large Force will terrify, and engage many to join you, a middling one will encourage Resistance, and gain no Friends." Thus he wrote on November 2 to Lord Barrington.

He was shocked by the behavior of the Continental Congress, for he had believed that that body would end in mere vaporing. He had revoked his call for a session of the Massachusetts legislature, but elections were held anyway and soon afterward the members of the assembly began to gather at Salem, forming themselves into a provincial congress.

Samuel Adams, back from Philadelphia, was busy with plans for a bang-up celebration of the fifth anniversary of the Boston Massacre. To hold such a meeting in Boston in 1775 would be not only illegal but perilous. The soldiers, though sternly disciplined, had been jeered beyond measure and could stand just so much.

The two dangerous posts, the occupants of which would in effect be offering themselves as possible martyrs on the altar of freedom, were the chairmanship of the memorial meeting and the oratory. Dr. Joseph Warren was to be the orator, Samuel Adams the chairman.

March 5 would have been the exact anniversary of the Massacre, but since it fell on a Sunday, the memorial meeting was held on March 6, a Monday, in the Old South Church.

There were almost forty British officers in the audience. Were they looking for trouble? Samuel Adams did not try to put them out, but instead went down to the floor and thanked them for coming. He would give them better seats, he said, and he placed them on the pulpit steps, so that they faced the rest of the crowd, which numbered slightly over two thousand.

Dr. Warren, a florid speaker always, did not pull his oratorical punches. It was as "hot" a speech as anybody in Boston had ever heard. Once, goaded beyond restraint, a few of the British officers cried, "Fie! Fie!" and some men in the back of the church, who thought they had heard the words "Fire! Fire!" started a rush for the doors. But an alert chairman soon restored order.

Soon after this meeting, however, Samuel Adams *did* get out of town, and barely in time.

CHAPTER TWENTY-SIX

They Came with the Dawn

On March 30, 1775, the Massachusetts provincial congress, meeting now at Concord, resolved that "whenever the Army under command of General Gage, or any part thereof to the Number of Five Hundred, shall march out of the Town of Boston, with Artillery and Baggage," it should be attacked.

Big words, but the Tories did not believe that the Whigs would see it through. At the same time the Whigs did not believe that the Tories would stick it out.

There was a spate of discussion as to why General Gage had not descended in force upon that memorable memorial meeting at the Old South Church, when he might have netted not only Dr. Warren and Samuel Adams but also a cartful of lesser Patriot leaders. More reinforcements were on the way, as he knew. Why then did he not stall even longer? Why did he make his move as early as April?

There are several possible answers to this question. Gage might have taken overseriously the reports that reached him about militia activities inland, and knowing how slow London could be, he might have feared that his reinforcements would be delayed yet again until he was overwhelmingly outnumbered in America.

He might have sensed—he had received no official notice—that he was about to be relieved of command. He might have heard, however, that the *military* leadership, if not the governorship, had been offered to the hero of Montreal, Sir Jeffrey Amherst, who refused it.

Gage must have heard too, and this time officially, that three major generals, no less, had been assigned to the American theater, William Howe, Henry Clinton, and John Burgoyne. Gage knew his army, and he knew these generals, or at least he knew about them. They were pushers, climbers, ambitious officers all, members of Parliament with good family connections. Clinton was the grandson of an earl; Burgoyne had married a Stanley; while Howe, according to popular report, was a relative of royalty itself, if on the left-hand side. They were men who could be counted upon to grab all the glory there was to grab. Gage might well have decided to grab a little for himself before they arrived. It is not to his discredit that he took such things into consideration. He would not have survived if he hadn't. The British Army was a political institution.

On April 14 his mind was made up for him. That day H.M.S. *Nautilus* sailed into Boston Harbor bearing, among other things, an order from Lord Dartmouth. An intensely religious man, Dartmouth at first had been classed as a friend of America, but the Tea Party had hardened him, and now he reported the feeling among the King's ministers, who clamored for action. Dartmouth was gentlemanly about it. He realized, as always, that Gage, being on the scene, was in a better position to know what was needed, and he made allowance for the fact that his letter would be at least five or six weeks on the way. He did not issue a *direct* order. But his meaning was clear. Gage should get busy.

Two days later, on April 16, Gage did move. He asked Admiral Grave to lend him some landing craft, and Grave complied with alacrity. No one was to know what these boats were for.

Gage instructed his second in command, Lord Percy, to have the grenadiers and light infantry companies of all regiments prepared to march the night of April 18, with a full day's supply of food. Percy was not to accompany them, only to stand by in case of a call for help.

As the British Army was organized, two companies out of each infantry regiment were made up of picked men, and these were called the flank companies, because on parade their position was in fact on the flanks. The grenadiers, who no longer carried grenades, were tall, burly men. The light infantry were fast fellows. Together, they made up an elite corps, the flankers, the scouts, the advance guards. When these soldiers, the cream of the army, were segregated from the ordinary infantrymen and gathered into a separate force, people might talk. General Gage just had to take this chance.

In charge of the expedition was Lieutenant Colonel Francis Smith, who won the post because of his seniority. Smith was steady, but deplorably slow. His second in command was, unexpectedly, a marine, Major John Pitcairn.

Worcester had briefly tempted General Gage, for it was known that the Patriots had collected large supplies there. But Worcester was almost forty miles away. If the force at Boston had included a regiment of horse—not heavy horse, not battle cavalry, but dragoons, mounted infantrymen—this would have served the purpose. Such a regiment was on the way, Gage knew, but he conceived himself to be under orders to strike immediately. Therefore, he would march to Concord. The supplies that had been gathered there were not mountainous, like those at Worcester, but they would constitute a good prize. There was the additional inducement that on the way to Concord, which was twenty-three miles from Boston, the men might pick up those two archrebels, Samuel Adams and John Hancock, who were known to be skulking in those parts.

The same thought had occurred to the Patriots, and when they noted the preparation of the landing craft, they took steps to warn Hancock and Adams.

The only question was whether Gage would send his men across the Neck, which would mean marching them through Roxbury and Cambridge, towns strongly Whiggish, or whether he would save a few miles by using those landing barges to ferry them across Back Bay, a little over a mile of shallow, brackish water—though the poet was to call it "by sea"—to rural East Cambridge, where there was nobody to observe them. From there they could easily reach the Menotomy-Lexington-Concord road. The barges, after all, might be a false clue.

The Patriots themselves did both. When the hush-hush was at its height—muffled oarlocks, whispered commands, all the rest—Dr. Warren, unmolested still in his Boston office, sent out William Dawes, Jr., to ride across the Neck and up through Cambridge to Lexington and Concord, raising the militia as he went. The Neck was supposed to be sealed after dark, but Dawes, no tyro, made it.

About half an hour later Paul Revere reported to Dr. Warren, who sent him north across the Charles River, under the very guns of *Somerset*, the largest warship in those waters, to Charlestown. A rowboat had been hidden near the foot of the Common for this trip, and a good horse, already saddled, was waiting in Charlestown.

Dawes would have 16 61/88ths miles to go; Revere, a much older man, 12 86/88ths miles. Dawes's route was the more populous, and since he started sooner and ended later, going farther, it is certain that he awakened more militiamen than did Paul Revere.

Not only did these riders get out of Boston ahead of the red-coats, but the latter were held up, knee-deep in muck and cold water, at Lechmere Point in East Cambridge for more than an hour and a half until their rations caught up with them.

By the time the column, numbering about 500, got under way, church bells were ringing ahead of them, and though it was still dark, all Middlesex County was astir.

Revere got to Lexington first. He conferred for a little while with the militiamen under John Parker, who were gathering on the green, and then he rode a few hundred yards out the Bedford road to the home of the village pastor, Reverend Jonas Clark, John Hancock's cousin. In that house, besides the pastor himself, there were sleeping John Hancock and Samuel Adams, who had been making final preparations before they started for Philadelphia and the first sitting of the *Second* Continental Congress. Also there were Mrs. Thomas Hancock, John's aunt, the widow of the man who had made all the money, and John's fiancée, Miss Dorothy Quincy.

A guard of eight militiamen surrounded the manse, and their sergeant hissed at the rider now, begging him not to make any noise.

"Noise!" cried Revere. "You'll have noise enough before long! The regulars are coming out!"

Hancock himself overheard this, and begged Revere to come in. The other messenger, Dawes, arrived a few minutes later.

Hancock was feverishly excited. He polished his pistol and flourished his sword. He would go down to the green and meet the British single-handed, if need be. Samuel Adams tut-tutted this. Battle, Adams pointed out, was not for them. They belonged to "the cabinet."

Dawes and Revere, back on the Lexington common, where the shivering mustketeers waited, took up with a young physician from Concord, who had been sparking a local girl and was about to start home. Dr. Prescott was a dedicated Patriot, and he would be useful along the five miles between the towns, for he knew everybody there.

They did not get far. A group of British officers, sent out for just this purpose, arrested them. Prescott, the best mounted, got away, and a little later Dawes also broke loose and outrode his pursuers. But the British held on to Paul Revere until the shooting was over. He never did get to Concord.

Meanwhile Samuel Adams at last had succeeded in persuad-

ing the firebrand Hancock to run away. They went north,
across the fields in the direction of Woburn (now Burlington).

The British came to Lexington with the sunrise, rank on
smooth rank of them, a splendid sight. They had loaded their
guns down the road a piece. Which side fired first will never be
known, and it doesn't matter now. In minutes the redcoats
were marching off along the road to Concord, leaving eighteen
men dead and wounded on Lexington common, the rays of the
newly risen sun gilding their blood.

Adams and Hancock were almost two miles away when
they heard the shots. They stopped.

It had happened.

"Oh, what a glorious morning this is," Adams cried.

Hancock thought he was talking about the weather.

CHAPTER TWENTY-SEVEN

"*The Storm Is Over*"

Only a fool would hurry a sunset. The glory of going slowly should not be hustled. Samuel Adams hadn't *burst* spectacularly upon the American political scene, but had wormed his way, inch by painful inch. He was to leave in much the same manner.

He liked Philadelphia well enough. Philadelphia, with a population of almost thirty thousand, was the largest city in the colonies, as it was the principal port. It had straight streets, most of them paved. It even had a system of garbage collection. Indeed, it was the municipal wonder of the New World, and when it was crowded with Congressional delegates, it also contained that most difficult of assets to define—good company. Yes, Adams liked Philadelphia. But of course it was not Boston.

Early in the course of the First Continental Congress Joseph Galloway, the shrewd lawyer and Franklin's protégé, had remarked upon the tirelessness of Samuel Adams and his amazing ability to keep the Boston political machine working smoothly even from far away. Well, it was not easy. The *Second* Continental Congress renewed itself time after time, staying in more or less continuous session. Meanwhile, Adams wrote and received innumerable letters. He kept the Caucus clubs in line. But he simply couldn't afford to go home often, and since his appeal had always been a personal one, the months in Pennsylvania were costing him power.

Yet to the rest of the world he *was* insurgent America, he was the very spirit of rebellion. When General Gage at last declared martial law for Massachusetts, he provided that anybody who had engaged in rebellious activity might be forgiven if he came in and signed an oath of allegiance to King George, *excepting* Samuel Adams and John Hancock, "whose offenses are of too flagitious a nature to admit of any other consideration than that of condign punishment." Cousin John Adams seemingly had not even been considered. Indeed, in 1778, when Cousin John was sent to Paris as the emergent nation's ambassador, he was hailed as the great revolutionist *Samuel* Adams, and when, miffed, he protested that he was not *Samuel* Adams, they cried, *"O, non, monsieur, c'est votre modestie!"* This is probably the only time that anybody ever called John Adams modest.

These two, like the other Massachusetts delegates, always kept in mind the need to quell the conservative fears of Southerners and especially of the Virginians.

There was a resounding gasp from the floor when at one of the first sessions Samuel Adams proposed that each meeting should be preceded by a prayer—and that each prayer should be given by a local *Episcopalian* minister. Everybody knew how he felt about bishops and synods and such. The thing was done, of course, in the name of unity, for Virginia was solidly Episcopalian.

A Massachusetts man, John Hancock, who wanted the job, was in the chair when the matter of appointing a commander in chief of the new Continental Army came up. John Adams rose to make a nomination. Hancock leaned forward, looking grave but receptive. John Adams proposed the name of a member of the Virginia delegation, Colonel George Washington. Hancock almost fell out of his chair. Samuel Adams promptly seconded the nomination.

Unity, unity.

John Adams was a member of the committee to announce

independence, though he did little there except suggest a few minor changes in the first draft, written by Thomas Jefferson. Young Jefferson, a Virginian, had a high regard for both Adamses, but particularly for Samuel.

To Samuel, who had been working for this for so many years, the adoption of the Declaration of Independence must have been an anticlimax. Cannons were fired, bells were rung, the thing was read regiment by regiment to the Continental Army, which cheered, but Samuel Adams must have been wondering all the while why it had taken so long for his fellow countrymen to catch up to him.

Twelve of the thirteen colonies had bicameral governments —that is, they had two chambers in their legislative departments. Only one, Pennsylvania, had a unicameral government. This fascinated Samuel Adams, who looked upon it from the viewpoint of a political boss: It would be easier to centralize control of one house than to centralize control of two. When he served on the committee that framed the optimistically entitled Articles of Confederation and Perpetual Union, Samuel Adams saw to it that they called for a unicameral legislature. He did not get credit for the Articles of Confederation—that went to John Dickinson, the chairman of the committee—but there is no doubt that he was largely instrumental in framing them. With two such fine writers on the committee, it was no wonder that the Articles succeeded in saying all that they had to say in 2,850 words, though the Constitution, which replaced them, was to use almost 4,500, exclusive of captions and amendments.

The Articles of Confederation have been sneered at as weak, but they did prevent the colonies from falling apart at a critical juncture; they bridged a gap. Parenthetically, it was the Articles that gave the nation its name: The United States of America.

Between November, 1777, and May, 1778, Samuel Adams

was secretary of state of Massachusetts, though he could not afford to spend much time there. He was also a member of the Massachusetts board of war. Late in 1779 the province—it was one of the last to do so—got around to organizing itself as a sovereign state. Samuel Adams was a member of the convention that framed the constitution, but he was too ill at the time to do much, too ill even to fight successfully for his own proposal of a unicameral legislature. He was called upon at least to frame Article III, the religious article, which he did. The result was the strictest, narrowest such article in the land, a monument of bigotry calculated to give Quakers, Baptists, Episcopalians, and all other such non-Congregationalists a hard time. *Political* liberty Samuel Adams approved; *religious* liberty, no.

He stuck with the Second Continental Congress to the end, and was one of the very few who did so. In April of 1781, when its business was finished at last, he left Philadelphia, to be elected president of the new state senate.

A few years earlier no one in Massachusetts would have dreamed of anybody but Samuel Adams as the first elected governor. But he had lost touch with people. Because of his work in the congress he had not been able to keep up old Boston contacts, much less make any new ones, as John Hancock had done. Hancock had gone out for the job early and with determination. The presidency of the Continental Congress gave him prestige, though very little work, so that he was able to spend more time in Boston than in Philadelphia, something that Samuel Adams could not afford. Adams, as election day neared, falteringly asked Hancock for the *lieutenant* governorship. This request was refused.

Samuel sold the moldering pile in Purchase Street, and bought a three-story, more or less yellow, depressing house in Winter Street, a part of the confiscated estate of a Tory, Sylvanus Gardiner. The price was £1,000, all mortgage. He and Betsy lived there with Surry the ex-slave, and Hannah,

Samuel's daughter, and her husband and their children. They still said grace before each meal and had an evening prayer service every night after dinner, and they went to church, as a body, twice every Sunday.

Samuel Adams, Jr., a surgeon, who had died in the service of the Continental Army, left claims against the government amounting to $6,000, and after a lot of trouble, the father was able to collect these claims. Before that, he speculated in real estate, buying lots in the Jamaica Plain section near Boston, and did very well.

He refused to become a delegate to the Constitutional convention in Philadelphia in 1787. He knew that it would be overwhelmingly Federalist, which he couldn't stand.

He was in his seventies now, but he wore glasses only for reading. He was the Old Patriot, a familiar figure in Boston, with his florid baby cheeks, his bright blue eyes. He never shuffled. He was erect, infallibly polite, a man of dignity.

Feelings about the French Revolution—this was before the Reign of Terror—were strong. Samuel Adams was pro-French, but not to the point where he would wear his own hair or those newfangled long trousers and split-tailed coats, themselves signs of republicanism. He still wore an old-fashioned tiewig and knee breeches.

He ran for Congress from the Suffolk County district, against an unknown young lawyer from Dedham, Fisher Ames, and lost.

He ran as an elector pledged to oppose the nomination of his cousin as second President of the United States in 1786. He lost that too.

This was the man who a little while ago had led John Hancock around "like an ape." Hancock had the executive's job sewed up. Not until 1789 did he give the Old Patriot a nod, so that Samuel Adams was elected lieutenant governor.

The post carried with it no power and no pay, which did not trouble Adams, though he had not yet collected on his son's claims and was now destitute. Some friends got together and pushed through the legislature a bill authorizing a £500-a-year salary for the lieutenant governor.

Hancock died in 1793, and Samuel Adams automatically became governor. He was elected to this position in 1794, 1795, 1796, and 1797. He was having some trouble getting around now. He had followed Hancock's funeral wagon on foot, but not all the way.

The governorship paid £3,333 a year, but now he really didn't need the money.

Friends presented him with a coach and pair, complete with driver, but though he thanked them, and used the vehicle on certain state occasions, mostly he left it to Betsy.

He opposed the establishment of the Society of the Cincinnati as an opening wedge for military aristocracy. He opposed, and most bitterly, the legalization of stage plays in Massachusetts. When his veto of a bill permitting them was overridden, the Old Patriot shook a sad head. Boston, he was sure, was doomed. The Devil would take over.

In January of 1797 Adams had announced that at the end of his gubernatorial term he would retire from public life, and this he did. He could hardly read now, even with glasses. He returned the coach, horses, and driver to the public-spirited men who had given them to him as governor.

He had nothing to do. He was very unhappy.

He did live, at least, to see the election of Thomas Jefferson in 1800. That to him marked a turning point. "The storm is now over, and we are in port," he wrote Jefferson.

He died on October 2, 1803. It was a Sunday. He had been born on a Sunday, and he died on a Sunday.

For Further Reading

Most of Samuel Adams' surviving letters and papers, a great pile, are in the New York Public Library. Some of them, and certain others, were edited by Harry Alonzo Cushing, and published in four volumes by G. P. Putnam's Sons, New York, 1904–1908. These formed the principal source for this book, as they were the principal source for each of the previous biographies of this man:

Beach, Stewart, *Samuel Adams: The Fateful Years, 1764–1776*. New York: Dodd, Mead & Company, 1965.

Harlow, Ralph Volney, *Samuel Adams, Promoter of the American Revolution: A Study in Psychology and Politics*. New York: Henry Holt and Company, 1923.

Hosmer, James K., *Samuel Adams*. Boston: Houghton, Mifflin and Company, 1885.

Miller, John C., *Sam Adams, Pioneer in Propaganda*. Boston: Little, Brown and Company, 1936.

Wells, William Vincent, *The Life and Public Services of Samuel Adams*. 3 volumes. Boston: Little, Brown and Company, 1865.

The author enjoys writing biographies (this is his eighth), but he does not recommend them for the study of a given period of history, since biographies, even the so-called "debunking" ones, tend by their very nature to be one-sided, hero-worshipping works. The principal ones occasionally referred to in the preparation of the present book were the following:

Alden, John Richard, *General Gage in America, Being Principally a History of His Role in the American Revolution*. Baton Rouge, La.: Louisiana State University Press, 1948.

Allan, Herbert S., *John Hancock: Patriot in Purple*. New York: The Macmillan Company, 1948.

Bernhard, Winfred E. A., *Fisher Ames, Federalist and Statesman, 1758–1808*. Chapel Hill, N.C.: University of North Carolina Press, 1965.

Cary, John, *Joseph Warren: Physician, Politician, Patriot*. Urbana, Ill.: University of Illinois Press, 1964.

Crane, Verner Winslow, *Benjamin Franklin, Englishman and American*. Baltimore: Published for Brown University by Williams & Wilkins Company, 1936.

Forbes, Esther, *Paul Revere and the World He Lived In*. Boston: Houghton Mifflin Company, 1942.

Freeman, Douglas Southall, *George Washington: a Biography*. 6 volumes. New York: Charles Scribner's Sons, 1948–54.

French, Allen, *General Gage's Informers: New Material upon Lexington and Concord, Benjamin Thompson as Loyalist and the Treachery of Benjamin Church, Jr.* Ann Arbor, Mich.: The University of Michigan Press, 1932.

Frothingham, Richard, *The Life and Times of Joseph Warren*. Boston: Little, Brown and Company, 1910.

Hosmer, James K., *The Life of Thomas Hutchinson, Royal Governor of the Province of Massachusetts Bay*. Boston: Houghton, Mifflin and Company, 1896.

Morse, John T., *John Adams*. Boston: Houghton, Mifflin and Company, 1899.

Namier, Lewis, *Charles Townshend: His Character and Career*. Cambridge, England: Cambridge University Press, 1959.

Sabine, Lorenzo, *Biographical Sketches of Loyalists of the American Revolution*. 2 volumes. Boston: Little, Brown and Company, 1864.

Stille, Charles J., *The Life and Times of John Dickinson, 1732–1808*. Philadelphia: Historical Society of Pennsylvania, 1891.

Taylor, Emerson, *Paul Revere*. New York: Edward Valentine and Dodd, Mead & Company, 1930.

Tyler, Moses Coit, *Patrick Henry*. Boston: Houghton Mifflin Company, 1898.

Van Doren, Carl, *Benjamin Franklin*. New York: The Viking Press, 1938.

Washburn, Charles G., *Jasper Maudit, Agent in London for the Province of Massachusetts-Bay, 1762-1765*. 2 volumes. Boston: The Massachusetts Historical Society, 1917, 1925.

The standard histories of the American Revolution—Trevelyan, Alden, Gordon, Botta, Ward, Fiske, Stedman, French, Fisher, Frothingham, Jameson, Mackesy, Peckham, Perkins, Ramsey, etc., etc.—all contain at least forewards or first chapters on a question that increasingly is fascinating historians, "How did it all start?" For more specific, more detailed stud-

ies of the origin and preliminaries of that monumental con-
test, the following (of which the last-named, the Zobel book,
is particularly recommended) are available:

Andrews, Charles M., *The Colonial Period of American History*. 4
volumes. New Haven, Conn.: Yale University Press, 1967.
Bailyn, Bernard, *The Ideological Origins of the American Revolution*.
Cambridge, Mass.: Harvard University Press, 1967.
Becker, Carl, *The Eve of the Revolution: A Chronicle of the Breach
with England*. New Haven, Conn.: Yale University Press, 1918.
Beer, George Louis, *British Politics and the American Revolution: The
Path to War, 1773–75*. New York: The Macmillan Company, 1907.
————, *The Commercial Policy of England toward the American Col-
onies*. New York: Columbia University Press, 1893.
Davidson, Philip, *Propaganda and the American Revolution, 1763–1783*.
Chapel Hill, N.C.: University of North Carolina Press, 1941.
Dickerson, Oliver Morton, *American Colonial Government, 1696–1765:
A Study of the British Board of Trade in Its Relation to the Amer-
ican Colonies, Political, Industrial, Administrative*. Cleveland, Ohio:
The Arthur H. Clark Company, 1912.
————, *The Navigation Acts and the American Revolution*. Philadel-
phia: University of Pennsylvania Press, 1951.
Ford, Worthington Chauncey, *Boston in 1775*. Brooklyn, N.Y.: His-
torical Printing Club, 1892.
French, Allen, *The Day of Concord and Lexington: The Nineteenth of
April, 1775*. Boston: Little, Brown and Company, 1925.
Gipson, Lawrence Henry, *The Coming of the Revolution, 1763–1775*.
New York: Harper & Brothers, 1954.
Granger, Bruce Ingham, *Political Satire in the American Revolution,
1763–1783*. Ithaca, N.Y.: Cornell University Press, 1960.
Hansen, Harry, *The Boston Massacre: An Episode of Dissent and Vio-
lence*. New York: Hastings House, 1970.
Hawkes, James A., *Retrospect of the Boston Tea-Party*. New York:
S. S. Bliss, 1834.
Hinkhouse, Fred Junkin, *The Preliminaries of the American Revolution
as Seen in the English Press*. New York: Columbia University Press,
1926.
Howard, George Elliott, *Preliminaries of the Revolution, 1763–1775*.
New York: Harper & Brothers, 1905.
Hunt, Agnes, *The Provincial Committees of Safety of the American
Revolution*. Cleveland, Ohio: Western Reserve University Press, 1904.
Jameson, J. Franklin, *The American Revolution Considered as a Social
Movement*. Boston: The Beacon Press, 1961.
Kidder, Frederic, *History of the Boston Massacre, March 5, 1770*. Al-
bany, N.Y.: Joel Munsell, 1870.

Knollenberg, Bernhard, *Origin of the American Revolution, 1759–1766.* New York: The Macmillan Company, 1960.

Labaree, Benjamin Woods, *The Boston Tea Party.* New York: Oxford University Press, 1964.

———, *The Road to Independence, 1763–1776.* New York: The Macmillan Company, 1963.

Labaree, Leonard Woods, *Royal Government in America: A Study of the British Colonial System before 1783.* New York: Frederick Ungar Publishing Company, 1958.

Lacy, Dan, *The Meaning of the American Revolution.* New York: New American Library, 1964.

Main, Jackson Turner, *The Social Structure of Revolutionary America.* Princeton, N.J.: Princeton University Press, 1965.

Miller, John C., *Origins of the American Revolution.* Boston: Little, Brown and Company, 1948.

Morgan, Edmund S., *The Birth of the Republic, 1763–89.* Chicago: University of Chicago Press, 1956.

Morgan, Edmund S. and Helen M., *The Stamp Act Crisis: Prologue to Revolution.* Chapel Hill, N.C.: University of North Carolina Press, 1953.

Murdock, Harold, *The Nineteenth of April, 1775.* Boston: Houghton Mifflin Company, 1923.

Rossiter, Clinton, *Seedtime of the Republic: The Origin of the American Tradition of Political Liberty.* New York: Harcourt, Brace and Co., 1953.

Schlesinger, Arthur Meier, *Prelude to Independence: The Newspaper War on Britain.* New York: Alfred A. Knopf, Inc., 1958.

Shy, John, *Toward Lexington: The Role of the British Army in the American Revolution.* Princeton, N.J.: Princeton University Press, 1965.

Sosin, Jack M., *Agents and Merchants: British Colonial Policy and the Origins of the American Revolution, 1763–1775.* Lincoln, Neb.: University of Nebraska Press, 1965.

Tyler, Moses Coit, *The Literary History of the American Revolution.* 2 volumes. New York: G. P. Putnam's Sons, 1897.

Van Tyne, Claude Halstead, *The Causes of the War of Independence.* Boston and New York: Houghton Mifflin Company, 1922.

Warren, James, *Warren-Adams Letters: Being Chiefly a correspondence among John Adams, Samuel Adams, and James Warren.* 2 volumes. Boston: The Massachusetts Historical Society, 1917, 1925.

Zobel, Hiller B., *The Boston Massacre: The Fateful Confrontation on King Street, March 5, 1770, the Events that led to it, and the Aftermath in a Colony moving toward Revolution.* New York: W. W. Norton and Company, Inc., 1970.

In matters ecclesiastical the books most frequently consulted were as follows:

Baldwin, Alice Mary, *The New England Clergy and the Revolution.* Durham, N.C.: Duke University Press, 1928.
Coupland, Reginald, *The Quebec Act: A Study in Statesmanship.* Oxford, England: The Clarendon Press, 1925.
Cross, A. L., *The Anglican Episcopate and the American Colonies.* New York: Longmans, Green and Co., 1902.
Davidson, Elizabeth H., *The Establishment of the English Church in the Continental American Colonies.* Durham, N.C.: Duke Univisity Press, 1936.
Dunning, Albert E., *Congregationalists in America.* New York: J. A. Hill & Co., 1894.
Hart, Gerald E., *The Quebec Act, 1774.* Montreal, Que.: Society for Historical Studies, 1891.
Headley, J. T., *The Chaplains and Clergy of the Revolution.* New York: Charles Scribner, 1864.
Manross, William Wilson, *A History of the American Episcopal Church.* New York and Milwaukee: Morehouse Publishing Company, 1935.
Metzger, Charles H., *The Quebec Act: A Primary Cause of the American Revolution.* New York: The United States Catholic Historical Society, 1936.
Sweet, William Warren, *Religion in Colonial America.* New York: Charles Scribner's Sons, 1942.
Thornton, John Wingate, *The Pulpit of the American Revolution.* Boston: Gould and Lincoln, 1860.
Tiffany, C. C., *A History of the Protestant Episcopal Church in the United States of America.* New York: Charles Scribner's Sons, 1899.

Since it is always well to learn about the other side, the following more or less pro-British books are suggested:

Adams, Randolph Greenfield, *Political Ideas of the American Revolution: Britannic-American Contribution to the Problem of Imperial Organization, 1765–1775.* Durham, N.C.: Trinity College Press, 1922.
Barker, John, *The British in Boston, Being the Diary of Lieutenant John Barker of the King's Own Regiment From November 15, 1774, to May 31, 1776,* with notes by Elizabeth Ellery Dana. Cambridge, Mass.: Harvard University Press, 1924.
Barnes, D. G., *George III and William Pitt.* Stanford, Calif.: The Stanford University Press, 1939.
Brown, Gerald Saxon, *The American Secretary: The Colonial Policy*

of Lord George Germain, 1775–1778. Ann Arbor, Mich.: University of Michigan Press, 1963.

Brown, Weldon A., *Empire or Independence: A Study in the Failure of Reconciliation, 1774–1783*. Baton Rouge, La.: Louisiana State University Press, 1941.

Butterfield, Herbert, *George III and the Historians*. New York: The Macmillan Company, 1950.

Champion, Richard, *The American Correspondence of a Bristol Merchant, 1766–1776*. Edited by G. H. Guttridge. Berkeley, Calif.: University of California Press, 1934.

Channing, Edward, and Coolidge, Archibald Cary, editors. *The Barrington-Bernard Correspondence and Illustrative Matter, 1760–1770*. Cambridge, Mass.: Harvard University Press, 1912.

Clark, D. M., *British Opinion and the American Revolution*. New Haven, Conn.: Yale University Press, 1930.

Colbourn, H. Trevor, *The Lamp of Experience: Whig History and the Intellectual Origins of the American Revolution*. Chapel Hill, N.C.: University of North Carolina Press, 1965.

Coupland, Reginald, *The American Revolution and the British Empire*. London: Longmans, Green and Co., 1930.

Craven, Wesley Frank, *The Legend of the Founding Fathers*. New York: New York University Press, 1956.

Curtis, E. E., *The British Army in the American Revolution*. New Haven, Conn.: Yale University Press, 1926.

Donoughue, Bernard, *British Politics and the American Revolution: The Path to War, 1773–75*. London: Macmillan and Co., Ltd., 1964.

Fortescue, John William, *History of the British Army*. 10 volumes. New York: The Macmillan Company, 1899–1920.

Gage, Thomas, *The Correspondence of General Thomas Gage with the Secretaries of State, 1763–1775*. Compiled and edited by Clarence Edwin Carter. 2 volumes. New Haven, Conn.: Yale University Press, 1931.

Guttridge, G. H., *English Whiggism and the American Revolution*. Berkeley and Los Angeles: University of California Press, 1942.

Hargreaves, Reginald, *The Bloodybacks: The British Serviceman in North America and the Caribbean, 1655–1783*. New York: Walker and Company, 1968.

Hutchinson, Oliver, Andrew, et al., *Copy of Letters sent to Great Britain by his Excellency Thomas Hutchinson, the Hon. Andrew Oliver, and several other Persons, born and educated among us*. Boston: Edes and Gill, 1773.

Hutchinson, Peter Orlando, editor, *The Diary and Letters of His Excellency Thomas Hutchinson, Esq*. 2 volumes. Boston: Houghton Mifflin and Company, 1886.

Murdock, Harold, editor, *Concord Fight: being so much of the Narrative of Ensign Jeremy Lister of the 10th Regiment of the Foot as*

Pertains to his Services on the 19th of April, 1775, and to his Experiences in Boston during the Early Months of the Siege. Cambridge, Mass.: Harvard University Press, 1931.

Murray, Sir James, *Letters from America, 1773 to 1780.* Edited by Eric Robson. Manchester, England: Manchester University Press, 1951.

Namier, Lewis. *England in the Age of the American Revolution.* London: Macmillan and Company, Ltd., 1930.

Oliver, Peter, *Origin and Progress of the American Rebellion: A Tory View.* Edited by Douglass Adair and John A. Schutz. San Marino, Calif.: The Huntington Library, 1961.

Pares, Richard, *King George III and the Politicians.* New York: Oxford University Press, 1953.

————, *Yankees and Creoles: The Trade Between North America and the West Indies Before the American Revolution.* Cambridge, Mass.: Harvard University Press, 1952.

Ritcheson, Charles R., *British Politics and the American Revolution.* Norman, Okla.: University of Oklahoma Press, 1954.

Robson, Eric, *The American Revolution in Its Political and Military Aspects, 1763–1783.* London: The Batchworth Press, 1955.

Scull, G. D., editor, *The Montresor Journals.* New York: The New-York Historical Society, 1881.

Sosin, Jack M., *Whitehall and the Wilderness: The Middle West in British Colonial Policy, 1760–1775.* Lincoln, Neb.: University of Nebraska Press, 1961.

Van Tyne, Claude Halstead, *The Loyalists in the American Revolution.* New York: Peter Smith, 1929.

Wickwire, Franklin B., *British Subministers and Colonial America, 1763–1783.* Princeton, N.J.: Princeton University Press, 1966.

Winstanley, D. A., *Lord Chatham and the Whig Opposition.* Cambridge, England: Cambridge University Press, 1912.

Wrong, George M., *Canada and the American Revolution: The Disruption of the First British Empire.* New York: The Macmillan Company, 1935.

Index

DATE DUE

OC 30 '78			

GAYLORD